how we learn

Other Publications:

HUMAN BEHAVIOR

how we learn

BY LEE EDSON
AND THE EDITORS OF TIME-LIFE BOOKS

TIME-LIFE BOOKS, ALEXANDRIA, VIRGINIA

The Author: Lee Edson, a freelance writer and journalist specializing in science and medicine, has published articles in *The New York Times Magazine, Scientific American* and *Esquire.* A former program manager at Stanford Research Institute in Menlo Park, California, he is the author of *Worlds Around the Sun,* a book on planetary astronomy, and co-author of *The Wind and Beyond,* a biography of rocket scientist Theodore von Karman.

General Consultants for Human Behavior:
Robert M. Krauss is Professor of Psychology at Columbia University. He has taught at Princeton and Harvard and was Chairman of the Psychology Department at Rutgers. He is the co-author of *Theories in Social Psychology,* edits the *Journal of Experimental Social Psychology* and contributes articles to many journals on aspects of human behavior and social interaction.

Peter I. Rose, a specialist on racial and ethnic relations, is Sophia Smith Professor of Sociology and Anthropology at Smith College and is on the graduate faculty of the University of Massachusetts. His books include *They and We, The Subject Is Race* and *Americans from Africa.* Professor Rose has also taught at Goucher, Wesleyan, Colorado, Clark, Yale, Amherst, the University of Leicester in England, Kyoto University in Japan and Flinders University in Australia.

James W. Fernandez is Chairman of the Anthropology Department at Dartmouth College. His research in culture change has taken him to East, West and South Africa and the Iberian peninsula. Articles on his field studies have been widely published in European and American anthropology journals. He has been president of the Northeastern Anthropological Association and a consultant to the Foreign Service Institute.

Special Consultant for How We Learn:
Sam Glucksberg, Chairman of the Department of Psychology at Princeton University, is a specialist in developmental learning who is particularly interested in problem solving, memory and language use. He is a member of the Board of Editors for *Cognitive Psychology, Child Development* and the *Journal of Psycholinguistic Research,* and is co-author of *Experimental Psycholinguistics.*

Time-Life Books Inc.
is a wholly owned subsidiary of
TIME INCORPORATED

FOUNDER: Henry R. Luce 1898-1967

Editor-in-Chief: Hedley Donovan
Chairman of the Board: Andrew Heiskell
President: James R. Shepley
Vice Chairman: Roy E. Larsen
Corporate Editors: Ralph Graves,
Henry Anatole Grunwald

TIME-LIFE BOOKS INC.
MANAGING EDITOR: Jerry Korn
Executive Editor: David Maness
Assistant Managing Editors: Dale M. Brown,
Martin Mann, John Paul Porter
Art Director: Tom Suzuki
Chief of Research: David L. Harrison
Director of Photography: Robert G. Mason
Planning Director: Philip W. Payne (acting)
Senior Text Editor: Diana Hirsh
Assistant Art Director: Arnold C. Holeywell
Assistant Chief of Research: Carolyn L. Sackett

CHAIRMAN: Joan D. Manley
President: John D. McSweeney
Executive Vice Presidents: Carl G. Jaeger
(U.S. and Canada), David J. Walsh (International)
Vice President and Secretary: Paul R. Stewart
Treasurer and General Manager:
John Steven Maxwell
Business Manager: Peter G. Barnes
Sales Director: John L. Canova
Public Relations Director: Nicholas Benton
Personnel Director: Beatrice T. Dobie
Production Director: Herbert Sorkin
Consumer Affairs Director: Carol Flaumenhaft

HUMAN BEHAVIOR
Editorial Staff for *How We Learn:*
EDITOR: William K. Goolrick
Assistant Editor: Carole Kismaric
Text Editor: David S. Thomson
Designer: John Martinez
Assistant Designer: Marion Flynn
Staff Writers: Alice Kantor, Suzanne Seixas
Chief Researcher: Barbara Ensrud
Researchers: Susan Jonas, Jane Edwin,
Barbara Fleming, Dunstan Harris, Ruth Kelton,
Gail Nussbaum, Robin Richman, Heidi Sanford,
Jane Sugden

EDITORIAL PRODUCTION
Production Editor: Douglas B. Graham
Operations Manager: Gennaro C. Esposito
Assistant Production Editor: Feliciano Madrid
Quality Control: Robert L. Young (director),
James J. Cox (assistant),
Michael G. Wight (associate)
Art Coordinator: Anne B. Landry
Copy Staff: Susan B. Galloway (chief),
Charles Blackwell, Florence Keith, Celia Beattie
Picture Department: Dolores A. Littles,
Martin Baldessari

CORRESPONDENTS: Elisabeth Kraemer (Bonn);
Margot Hapgood, Dorothy Bacon (London);
Lucy T. Voulgaris (New York); Maria Vincenza
Aloisi, Josephine du Brusle (Paris); Ann Natanson
(Rome). Valuable assistance was also provided by:
Franz Spelman (Munich); Carolyn T. Chubet,
Miriam Hsia (New York); Craig Van Note
(Washington, D.C.).

Contents

The Role of Knowledge

At the turn of the 19th Century, swarms of sightseers converged on Paris to see what was heralded as the oddity of the era—a supposedly wild boy, half-human, half-animal, who had been captured in the woods of Aveyron in southern France. They came, it was said, not just to stare at a freak but to see what happens when a human being is removed from civilization at birth and left to survive only on his wits and the nuts and berries he can find. Would he prove to be the "noble savage" of Jean Jacques Rousseau, whose back-to-nature philosophy was still widely debated in France, or would he be something else?

For those who expected to see a delightfully natural youth the sight was a shock. The boy, it was reported, "was a degraded being, human only in shape; a dirty, scared, inarticulate creature, who trotted and grunted like the beasts of the fields, ate with apparent pleasure the most filthy refuse, was apparently incapable of attention or even of elementary perceptions such as heat or cold, and spent his time apathetically rocking himself backwards and forwards, like the animals at the zoo."

The Wild Boy of Aveyron, as he came to be known, might have been quickly forgotten had he not come to the attention of Jean-Marc-Gaspard Itard, a young French doctor who patiently devoted the next five years to teaching him the rudiments of civilized life. Itard named the youth Victor and developed ingenious techniques for his education—techniques, incidentally, that were subsequently adapted to the education of deaf mutes and the feeble-minded—but his efforts with Victor ended largely in frustration. The Wild Boy managed to dress himself and to learn a few commands, but his language comprised only a few syllables.

Whether the Wild Boy of Aveyron was truly wild or simply a retarded child who had become lost does not matter. He was unable to learn the way children the world over do, informally in their homes and formally in classrooms such as the Indian one shown at left, and so he remained largely an animal, lacking the essential qualities that distinguish civilized man from all other creatures.

Men are born with only a few innate abilities, the most obvious one being the reflex of sucking that enables the infant to gain nourishment. Almost everything else that makes a human being human is learned behavior, from the motor ability to walk fully erect to the complex nervous and muscular skills needed to fly a jet, from the first words a baby utters to the mastery of speaking and writing a language. Man's greatest distinction is his almost limitless ability to learn, to absorb and use the vast stores of knowledge created over the centuries by other human beings, and thus to master the world around him as no other creature on earth can. Man is preeminently the learning animal.

This does not mean that other animals are wholly without the ability to learn. Anybody who has ever owned a domestic pet knows that cats and dogs can learn a number of things. Circus-goers have seen seals that have learned to play musical instruments and elephants that can tap numbers with their feet. The power to learn, indeed, extends downward through the animal kingdom to some very lowly creatures. The earthworm has been taught by psychologists to move through a laboratory maze in search of food—although it is not smart enough to escape the fisherman digging for bait. The honeybee learns the landmarks that signify the places nectar can be gathered. Even fleas can learn to pull miniature wagons in that once-popular sideshow attraction, the flea circus. Laboratory rats learn how to do things that please researchers. The learning abilities of laboratory animals, in fact, have been of great help to psychologists in analyzing the learning mechanisms of all creatures, including man.

Beyond these laboratory achievements, the learning feats of some animals are truly impressive. Man's closest relative on the evolutionary ladder, the chimpanzee, possesses a remarkable ability to learn to communicate with man. The pharynx of chimpanzees is not sufficiently developed for them to approximate human speech, so their vocal repertoire is limited largely to grunts and squeaks. But they can learn various forms of sign language and speak with humans that way.

Some of the pioneering efforts in enabling chimps to communicate were made with a delightfully playful female chimp named Washoe. Washoe's trainers, Allen and Beatrice Gardner of the University of Nevada, patiently taught her words in the American Sign Language, a set of hand gestures used by deaf people. Over a four-year period, Washoe learned the signs for more than 160 words, a notable achievement for a chimpanzee. More impressive, she could generalize, that is, form concepts. If one of the Gardners pointed to a tree and made the gesture for "tree" in sign language, Washoe grasped the idea that the sign meant all trees and not just the one pointed to. Her trainers taught Washoe the sign for "open" by opening and closing doors. Washoe immediately applied the concept to all doors including the one on the refrigerator—plus containers of all sorts, bureau drawers and finally water faucets.

Still more impressive, Washoe could learn some syntax—that is, appropriate word orders. It was long assumed that this power, along with language use in general, was distinctly and exclusively human. If this were so, Washoe would have used the signs she had learned in random order. But better than 90 per cent of the time Washoe put her signs—her words

—in logical, intelligible sequences. One of her trainers reported a remarkable conversation with Washoe:

"She once pestered me for a cigarette I was smoking with a flurry of signs: 'Give me smoke,' 'Smoke Washoe,' 'Hurry give smoke,' and 'You give me smoke.' Since I do not approve of her smoking, I denied her requests. Finally, I signed to her, 'Ask politely.' She quickly responded with, 'Please give me that hot smoke.'"

Another trained chimp, Lucy, has in some ways outshone Washoe. Lucy frequently has made up original and appropriate combinations of word-signs. On one occasion Lucy was given a radish to eat. It was a hot one and burned Lucy's mouth. She immediately originated an eloquent description of a hot radish, combining the signs of her symbol language to complain: "cry hurt food."

But perhaps the champion chimp at communicating has been Lana. In experiments conducted at the Yerkes Primate Research Center in Atlanta, Georgia, she was placed in a plastic cube equipped with a computer console. The console had 75 keys, each with a geometric design that represented to Lana a word such as "food" or "come" or "open." Above the console was a lighted panel that showed Lana the symbols she had punched. Lana used the console almost constantly while awake to communicate with her trainers, who sat at another console with lighted panel outside the plastic cage. She was able to ask for food—"Lana want apple" —or that a window be opened so that she could look outdoors, or that one of the trainers come into the cube and play: "Tim tickle Lana." Her requests flashing on the trainers' panel, the trainers punched back their answers, which Lana then read on her panel. In other words, Lana carried on almost constant and lively conversations with her human keepers. Her knowledge of her symbol language advanced so far that if she punched out a sentence that contained an error, she would immediately hit the erase button and start over again.

But however gifted chimpanzees become in manipulating their symbolic languages, one fact remains—they have been taught the languages by man and did not invent them. Furthermore, without man's training, chimps have neither the desire nor the ability to learn any form of sign language more complicated than the usual chimp gesturing. This inability was highlighted by a rather pathetic episode involving Washoe. After seven years of language learning, Washoe was allowed by her trainers to go into semi-retirement and was placed in a commodious cage with other, untrained chimps. At first Washoe tried to communicate with these other simians, making her hand signs. But the other chimps never responded. They appeared to have no interest whatsoever in what Washoe was doing and were unable to perceive that her signs were an attempt at communication. In short, however intelligent chimps are, they cannot pass on sign language or other forms of human-style learning from one to another, from one generation to the next.

The same is true of another highly touted animal, the dolphin. Some of

the tales of the learning feats and language abilities of dolphins have made it sound as though they were potentially smarter than man. It is true that dolphins can be taught a large repertoire of clever and amusing tricks, as visitors to marinelands and aquariums are aware. For rewards of food, dolphins leap and dive and cavort in tanks, obeying quite complex instructions from their human trainers. The United States Navy has even trained dolphins to dive for and help retrieve practice torpedoes, and there are rumors that dolphins are taking their place in the shadowy world of international intrigue, trained to attach sensing devices to the hulls of rival nations' submarines.

Dolphins are such clever learners that it has seemed, for a while at least, that they might even enable man to fulfill the ancient dream of talking to an animal. Literature is full of examples of this long-held dream —the *Fables choisies* of the French poet La Fontaine; Dr. Doolittle, who had a wonderful ability to converse with a score of species; Alice's conversations with the Cheshire Cat, the White Rabbit and the Dormouse; and Tarzan's ability to talk to the apes. So scientists and the world of animal lovers were thrilled when it was discovered that dolphins have a wide repertoire of squeaks, grunts and whistles. Perhaps these noises when understood would turn out to be a full-blown language.

After much analysis, however, the experts have yet to crack the code of the dolphin language and the great hopes for the dolphin appear to be exaggerated. Russian researchers at the University of Moscow have reportedly compiled a dictionary of 400 dolphin squeaks, whistles and grunts, but they have little idea what most of them signify. Dr. John Lilly, a pioneer of dolphin research, claims that dolphins can understand human speech and even imitate some of its sounds. One of his dolphins, he claims, squeaked a recognizable "I love you" to one of Lilly's female assistants. But another expert, Forrest Wood, says flatly that "there is no good evidence that the dolphin approaches man in intelligence or even has anything comparable to human language."

The consensus seems to be that whatever language capability dolphins possess, it is rudimentary, and that the dolphin's brain, even though larger than a human's, is only slightly superior to an intelligent dog's. Most of the dolphin noises that have been construed to be highly sophisticated would appear to be merely echo-location signals, a sort of animal sonar that helps the dolphin navigate past obstacles in the water. Other noises are probably simple warnings. Each dolphin has a characteristic cry, a unique and self-identifying sound that the other dolphins in the same school recognize. Thus when a dolphin makes a beeping sound, it is saying, in effect, "This is Charlie talking and I'm over here to the left." Or in emergencies, "This is Charlie and danger is approaching." That, it would appear, is as complex as dolphin language gets.

Impressive as some of the learning feats of the dolphin and the chimp may be, they are puny by comparison with the accomplishments of man. Among many prodigious examples that can be drawn from any age and

Learning through the senses of sight and touch, a three-year-old on his first visit to The Cloisters museum in New York City examines a lifelike sculpture of a knight on a medieval tomb. Before touching the sculpture, the child had thought it would be warm and soft. He is startled to learn that it is cold and hard.

any country is Dr. Samuel Johnson, the towering "dictator" of English literature in the latter part of the 18th Century, who is perhaps more widely known today as the subject of James Boswell's great biography than for his own writings.

Of Johnson's many impressive achievements, the most remarkable perhaps was the dictionary—two thick volumes, the first major dictionary of the English language—that he compiled virtually singlehandedly. He chose the 40,000 currently used words that were to be defined in the dictionary and wrote all of the definitions himself, each meticulously differentiating the shades of meaning. These definitions remain unequaled for pungency and clarity. Moreover, Johnson determined the proper pronunciation of the words and also wrote their derivations, often relying on his own excellent knowledge of Greek, Latin and other languages. He also selected the 114,000 different quotations from literature that illustrated the various ways the words had been used by leading British writers of the previous two centuries.

Johnson originally planned to complete this mammoth task in three years. When a friend, Dr. William Adams, reminded him that the 40 members of the French Academy, an august scholarly body, had taken 40 years to compile a comparable dictionary of the French language, Johnson, with characteristically humorous bravado, replied, "forty times forty is sixteen hundred. As three to sixteen hundred, so is the proportion of an Englishman to a Frenchman."

As it turned out, the job took Johnson almost eight years—though during that time he also wrote more than 200 *Rambler* essays, many of them monuments of English prose, and the poem "The Vanity of Human Wishes," and did a host of literary odd jobs as well, to keep from starving. Eight years, considering the magnitude of the undertaking, is an incredibly short time. It took Noah Webster 20 years to do his pioneering American dictionary, in which he borrowed liberally from Johnson. The 10-volume *New English Dictionary*, also known as the *Oxford*, was compiled over a span of 44 years, from 1884 to 1928, with the help of no fewer than 1,300 scholars. Even this monumental work borrowed a number of Johnson's illustrative quotations. Johnson was not a trained lexicographer, but nevertheless he set the lexicographical standard for all subsequent dictionaries. His two volumes are one of the greatest scholarly achievements of all time. The conditions under which Johnson wrote it are eloquently described in the last lines of his preface to his great work:

"The *English Dictionary* was written with little assistance of the learned, and without any patronage of the great; not in the soft obscurities of retirement, or under the shelter of academic bowers, but amidst inconvenience and distraction, in sickness and in sorrow. . . . I may surely be content without the praise of perfection which, if I could obtain, in this gloom of solitude, what would it avail me? I have protracted my work till most of those whom I wished to please have sunk into the grave, and success and miscarriage are empty sounds; I therefore dismiss it with frigid tranquillity, having little to fear or hope from censure or from praise."

After the dictionary Johnson went on to produce a fine annotated edition of Shakespeare's works, with a long preface that is a milestone in English literary criticism, and short critical biographies of no fewer than 52 English poets, among many other works. But the dictionary was his greatest achievement of learning; what he had done was encompass the entire living English language of his era.

Modern times have produced other titans of learning. One of the great literary scholars of this century was the German Erich Auerbach. His wide-ranging mind comprehended world literature in virtually every era from the beginning of writing to the present. His masterwork, a book called *Mimesis*, contains impeccable critical essays on works as diverse as the Bible and Rabelais' *Gargantua and Pantagruel.* In each essay Auerbach worked with the text in its *original* language; to write *Mimesis* Auerbach had to have command of Hebrew, Greek, Latin, Dante's Italian, early and modern French, Spanish, English and, of course, his native German.

The 20th Century Irish writer James Joyce was both a creative genius and a man of vast, wide-ranging knowledge. He is said to have known at least the rudiments of a dozen languages and he was fluent in half a dozen. In his teens he became fascinated with Ibsen's plays and quickly taught

himself Norwegian so that he could read them in their original language. His knowledge of world literature was encyclopedic. He knew all the Greek and Latin Classics, was widely read in medieval mystical literature, became an authority on Aristotle, Dante, Shakespeare and Aquinas, and had a comprehensive and deep knowledge of French, Italian, Russian, German, English and American literature. He even knew popular literature and was acquainted with American comic strips: Mutt and Jeff turn up in a dream sequence in his great novel *Finnegans Wake.* It is perhaps not too great an exaggeration to say that he carried in his head the entire Western cultural tradition. He was without question the most erudite imaginative writer of modern times, as well as one of the most profound. One has to go back at least to Goethe to encounter a writer whose mind contained a comparable wealth of knowledge.

Less well known to the public, but remarkably learned nevertheless, was the American legal scholar Roscoe Pound. Gifted with a phenomenal memory, Pound as a boy in Sunday school could recite an entire chapter of the Bible after one reading. He entered the University of Nebraska, his home state, at age 14, graduated at 18 and received his Masters Degree in botany at 19. He attended Harvard Law School for one year—the normal law course is three years—and was admitted to the bar at age 20.

Pound then simultaneously practiced law, taught it at Nebraska's law school and worked for his Ph.D. degree in botany, directing in the meanwhile a botanical survey of his native state. After some years of teaching at several law schools, he went to Harvard in 1910 and became dean of its law school in 1916. During two decades as dean, Pound revolutionized the teaching of law and was a major influence in changing modern legal philosophy. At one time or another he taught virtually every course the law school offered. He wrote 44 books and some 1,000 papers and pamphlets. Meanwhile he taught himself Sanskrit, Greek, Latin, Hebrew, French, German, Italian, Spanish and some Russian. During World War II, when many teachers had gone into the service, Pound helped out by teaching the classics in Harvard College. After his retirement from teaching in 1947 at age 76, he taught himself Chinese—one of the most difficult of all languages to learn—and codified the laws of China for the Nationalist government. But one of his loves was always botany and he remained proud of the fact that he had discovered a rare lichen that is named, appropriately, *roscoepoundia.*

Intellectual giants such as Pound, Joyce, Auerbach and Johnson are something more than examples of man's remarkable ability to acquire knowledge. They are, in addition, symbols of his unique ability to preserve that knowledge and pass it along from one generation to the next. For man alone has succeeded in accumulating great stores of information, ideas, techniques and inventions and in developing methods for transmitting this body of knowledge to his successors. Man alone has discovered how to create continuity of learning so that his species might not only survive but also build civilizations on what he has learned.

Through a large part of man's history, knowledge was transmitted orally from one generation and one individual to the next. The *Iliad* and the *Odyssey*, scholars say, were originally preserved through oral tradition. The stories making up the epics had been told for a couple of centuries before a blind poet from Asia Minor named Homer organized them into two great poems. The poems were remembered and repeated by professional storytellers, and thus passed on to generation after generation for several more centuries until they were at last written down. In similar fashion, much of the Old Testament was passed on orally for hundreds of years before being recorded on clay tablets. Likewise, in centuries past when the vast majority of the people of even the most advanced nations were illiterate, bards and minstrels and strolling actors disseminated the culture's folk tales, myths and heroic legends. Cultures that preserve their central traditions and tales by passing them on orally persist today in many parts of the world. Some 3,000 languages are spoken worldwide; only 5 per cent of them have a written form.

That 5 per cent, however, has accounted for a veritable explosion of information. In the last several centuries, the world of preserved knowledge

An international gallery of prodigies

The average man learns a staggering amount about the world around him over his lifetime. But through history there have been a few persons with an extraordinary ability to master knowledge. The five whose pictures appear at right were among the most prodigious learners who ever lived. They range from a 10th Century Islamic physician, Avicenna, to a 19th Century English economist, John Stuart Mill.

Avicenna is the Latinized name of Ibn Sina, a Persian who lived from 980 to 1037. His most notable achievement was the Canon of Medicine, a medical encyclopedia so advanced that it was used for five centuries. Ibn Sina wrote some 150 other books on such varied subjects as philosophy, mathematics, theology and astronomy. Like many learned men, he got off to a fast start: he is said to have memorized the Koran by age 10 and to have been physician to a sultan at 18.

Giovanni Pico della Mirandola was a prodigy even among the great Humanist scholars of the 15th Century. At 17 Pico was already deep into the works of Aristotle as well as the Hebrew and Arabic languages. By 23 he was master of so many areas of philosophy and religion that he drew up a list of 900 topics and challenged the scholars of Europe to debate him on any or all of them. Before his death at 31 he had assembled one of Europe's great libraries.

has expanded to such a degree that no human mind—even that of a Pound, a Joyce, an Auerbach or a Johnson—could possibly encompass it all.

Yet the ordinary person absorbs an amazing amount of knowledge nowadays. In the course of a lifetime he accumulates a vocabulary of more than 50,000 words; in many countries—especially in Europe—he learns at least one language in addition to his own and sometimes two or three. He learns not only to talk, but also to read and write, to measure and calculate and to express abstract thoughts. Even in high school modern-day students are taught as a matter of course scientific theories that go far beyond the knowledge or understanding of Aristotle or Isaac Newton.

Beyond this, most people automatically acquire impressive mechanical and physical skills, although many of them—such as the dexterity required to drive a modern car in traffic—are taken for granted. To take a very different example, consider the numerous skills that Asian farmers must learn to properly terrace and irrigate fields of rice and then to successfully plant and harvest the crop.

Consider, too, that most people at one time or another learn to play a sport, sometimes several of them. It seemed for years that only people

Denis Diderot, 18th Century French philosopher and man of letters, served as principal editor of the 28-volume Encyclopédie, the most ambitious collection of knowledge that had been undertaken up to his day. He wrote hundreds of the articles himself. In addition, he produced three extraordinary novels, plays, influential articles on art and other works revealing knowledge of neurophysiology, biology, chemistry, poetry, linguistics and esthetics.

Johann Wolfgang von Goethe, who lived from 1749 to 1832, was the greatest of German poets as well as a scientist. By age 16 he had already written religious poems, a novel and a prose epic. While continuing to write, he studied both law and medicine. Invited to live in the duchy of Saxe-Weimar by its ruler, Goethe became minister of state and educated himself in agriculture, horticulture and mining. He then proceeded to master anatomy, biology, optics and mineralogy.

It has been said that John Stuart Mill, the 19th Century English economist and philosopher, knew more at 13 than most people learn in their entire lives. He began reading Greek at age three and Latin at seven and had devoured all the masterpieces in both languages by 12. He then turned to logic and political economy; by 17 he was writing articles for the Westminster Review. Among his great and varied works are The Principles of Political Economy and On Liberty.

born in North America north of the 49th parallel—i.e., Canadians—could master hockey, but now the game has become international. Czechs and Russians, among many others, learn the difficult combinations of physical and mental skills that hockey requires: to skate and handle the puck flawlessly without being conscious of what the hands and feet are doing, and to comprehend instantly the changing flow of the play. Men the world over, for that matter, are skilled in that truly international game, soccer, which requires both overall coordination and extreme agility.

A great deal of this learning goes on outside the school, even though when people speak of learning, their minds generally picture a classroom. A large part of the information and the techniques that all people must master in order to survive are learned in the home or in normal daily contact with other humans. The normal child learns many of life's most necessary lessons very early, long before kindergarten. The most remarkable, surely, is the ability to start speaking a language. Then there is—to the child —the baffling complexity of the world around him: Why is the sky blue, and what does grass come from, and how do doors work, and windows, and stairs, and chairs, and stoves, and knives and forks, and buttons and zippers, and coats and gloves? The list of things the child must learn in a few short years is virtually endless—which makes more understandable the three-year-old's endless reiteration of his favorite word: "Why?"

The importance of home learning in the early years cannot be exaggerated. That is why much of this book on how humans learn concentrates on childhood learning. Seeing how and why the child is impelled to learn is perhaps the most interesting part of the entire subject.

But nonschool learning does not cease when the child grows into a young adult. As we all know, learning goes on throughout life, right into old age. The adage that "you can't teach an old dog new tricks" has been disproved by studies and observations of the aged. The Israeli success, for instance, in bringing into their country the old people of Europe and teaching them a new language, Hebrew, has demonstrated the learning potential of the elderly. "I grow old," said the Athenian statesman Solon, "learning something new every day." Associate Justice Oliver Wendell Holmes of the U.S. Supreme Court was found reading Plato at age 90. "Why?" he was asked. "To improve my mind," was the reply.

How men could possibly learn all the things that are required merely to exist, to say nothing of the extra skills that make life more comfortable or more enjoyable, has baffled philosophers and scientists through the ages. Plato and Aristotle both theorized about the subject, and so have many medieval and modern thinkers. A fundamental debate shaped up in the 18th Century between those who thought man came into the world gifted with innate ideas, and those who believed men were born with minds that were absolute blanks and that everything they learned came from experience.

The debate continues today, with some scientists holding that what man learns is entirely imposed from without, and others maintaining that the mind is more actively involved than that, creating a good deal of learning, so to speak, from within.

Most psychologists hew to a middle line, holding that while many behaviors are imposed on man by the environment, the mind itself is an active participant in learning. The two theories together, psychologists believe, account in large part for the ways in which people learn.

In the last half century or so, psychologists and other scientists have made substantial progress in answering the ancient question of why and how people learn. They now know much about the intellectual processes of the mind, and the creation of deeply held attitudes and responses. They have investigated the ways by which the mind stores learning and how it varies from culture to culture. Most important of all, they have found that with proper stimulation and incentive, there are virtually no limits to man's ability to learn. In designing man as a learning animal instead of enslaving him to the limited genetic endowment of the other species, nature gave him a unique gift—a capacity for building on the past and the means, if used properly, to advance himself and his culture indefinitely.

A lesson to suit every age

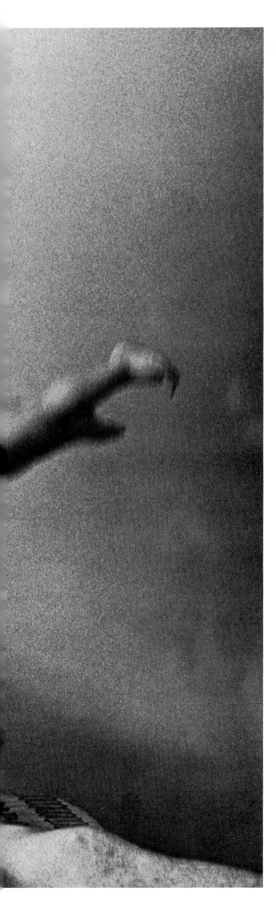

Tossed in the air by his loving father, a 10-month-old child is learning one of the most important lessons of early life: a basic confidence in his parents. Deprived of that security, the child might grow up emotionally crippled or unable to form affectionate bonds with others.

The human animal is a born learner who starts the educational process while he is kicking in his crib and does not stop until he dies. The newborn baby quickly learns that crying will bring him help, and his mother's presence means comfort and relief from hunger. In the months that follow, the child becomes a veritable learning machine, programed to master a rapid sequence of vital skills. He learns to crawl, walk, feed himself and talk.

By the end of his second year, the child has developed a vocabulary of around 200 words, and by the time he is six he has acquired a third of all his intellectual skills. In the adolescent years—13 to 20—the developing individual struggles with a tormenting problem as he learns to think and behave like an adult. Then, in early adulthood, both his perspective and his preoccupations shift. He becomes concerned with adjusting to a career, to his spouse and to his children; now he is involved with relating to other people.

Middle age brings one of life's most difficult problems: learning to accept one's lot and to reconcile oneself to the fact that all the hopes of youth are not going to be fulfilled. Then, with the onset of old age, productivity and motor skills slowly begin to decline—driving a car, for example, may become hazardous. But, contrary to widespread belief, a person's capacity for verbal comprehension, as well as his numerical and reasoning abilities, may increase well into old age. And some people, like the elderly couple shown on pages 30-31, who are both healthy and young in spirit, find that it is never too late to acquire new skills and to gain new satisfactions from life.

Childhood: exploring new worlds

A pair of four-year-olds, creating a house out of plastic tape, learn to explore the world outdoors and organize the space around them. The children like to imagine that the areas within the tape are closets and rooms. At this point their concentration is limited: they work at the task briefly and come back to it later.

Learning to play the piano, this seven-year-old has reached a fairly advanced stage in his intellectual development. His attention span has increased, and he can concentrate better and master more complex learning tasks than would have been possible a year or so earlier.

Adolescence: trying out adult roles

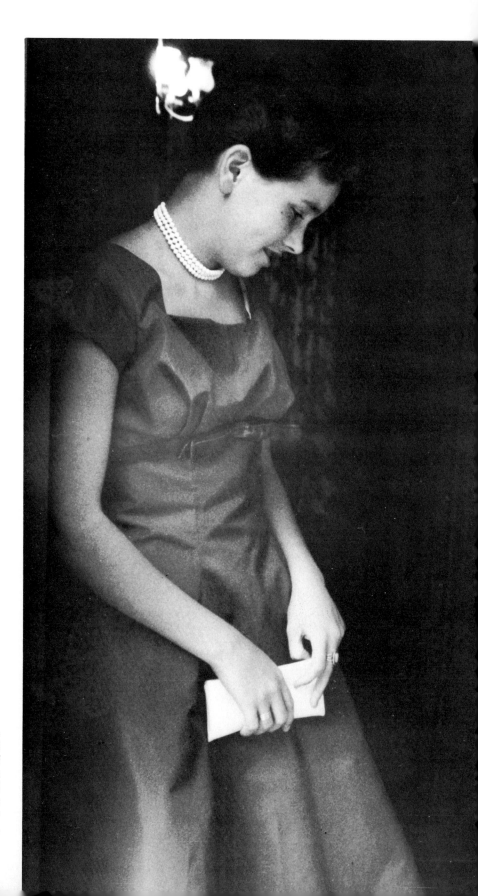

A pair of teenagers, all dressed up for their first date, betray the shyness and embarrassment that are characteristic of adolescents. This picture, shot for LIFE in 1956, reveals the self-doubt and uncertainty felt by the young couple as they begin to learn the roles they will play later on, when they are adults.

*A French father, helping his daughter
with her spelling while other members of
the family look on, is a learner as well
as a teacher. By involving himself with
the child's problems, he learns what
to expect of her under pressure and how
to relate to her more effectively. And in
the process he may improve his spelling.*

*A young Czech couple, sharing a moment
of intimacy, are poised on the threshold
of a difficult but rewarding period. At this
point they must learn a new way of life,
involving decisions about family size, life
styles and jobs. The problems are
formidable, but a study has shown that
older people look back on early adulthood
as the happiest time of their lives.*

Old age: never too late to learn

Trying out some steps in a lively folk dance they have just learned in a class at a Golden Age Club in New York, two frolicsome people offer proof that it is never too late to learn or to have fun. At this stage of life the ability to learn new skills depends on qualities these people have in abundance: good health, motivation and the will to enjoy life.

Behavior on Signal

2

On a bleak snow-clad Andes mountaintop the huddle of air-crash survivors faced death by starvation. They had finished the last morsels scavenged from the airplane's wrecked fuselage—a sliver of chocolate and a spoonful of jam per person. There were no lichens, roots or any other sort of vegetation on the snow-covered peak, and no animals. Hunger was so intense that many of the survivors sank toward apathy, losing their will to live. Then one of the survivors, a medical student named Roberto Canessa, suggested an appalling idea—that they eat the bodies of their 10 fellow passengers who had been killed in the crash. At first all the other survivors of the crash were horrified, but Canessa—coolly, scientifically—explained that all of them were dying of malnutrition and that cannibalism was the only alternative to death. Haltingly, painfully, overcoming enormous revulsion, the other survivors brought themselves to eat the human flesh that Canessa cured by drying it in the intense, high-altitude sunlight, although one boy named Numa Turcatti usually vomited after eating and often passed up his portion.

This harrowing tale, the actual experience of a group of South American air-crash victims, dramatizes the force possessed by what psychologists call conditioned learning responses that are deeply implanted in each individual by the society in which he grows up. There is nothing innately unhealthy or disgusting about human flesh; there is no physiological reason not to eat it. But people brought up in civilized societies have been taught by their cultures to loathe the very idea of eating it—even to the point of rejecting it through regurgitation. Such is the power that conditioned behavior can exert over everyone. It is the same sort of conditioning that makes a seasoned driver automatically hit the car's brake pedal when he sees a red light or a policeman's raised arm, or that makes a pedestrian mumble "pardon me" after accidentally bumping into a passerby. It is in large part through conditioning that the human organism learns the culturally approved ways to act.

The principles that determine how behavior is learned through conditioning were first discovered and understood through an epochal series of experiments with animals. The man credited with the discovery is Ivan Petrovich Pavlov, the Russian physiologist who did his far-reaching conditioning experiments between 1901 and 1936. Pavlov, born in 1849, the son of a poor country priest, studied for some years at a theological seminary. But in 1870, discovering a love for natural science, he transferred to St. Petersburg University, then a distinguished center for the study of physiology. After a decade and a half of preparation, he began the series of discoveries about the mechanisms of digestion that won him a 1904 Nobel Prize. Experimenting on dogs, he demonstrated how the gastric juices and other secretions, including those released by salivation, help the stomach to digest.

It was a serendipitous side effect of Pavlov's work on digestion that revolutionized the world of psychology. Pavlov ultimately became a hero in Soviet Russia and was rewarded and lionized by Lenin and Stalin. The basic message behind his psychological findings, that man as well as dog could be shaped and controlled by conditioning, supported the Marxist tenet that environment rather than heredity was crucial to human development. The Soviet government provided Pavlov with elaborate laboratory facilities where he refined his theories—looking in his long snowy beard more like the priest he might have been than a daring, innovative scientist —until his death at 86 in 1936.

Pavlov's psychological experiments originated when he noticed that his dogs began to salivate not only when their food was placed before them, but also when they heard the rattling of dishes or the footsteps of the caretaker who fed them. Pavlov set out to discover why this curious aspect of the digestive process took place. He rigged up a bell that rang just before the dog got its plate of food, and installed instruments to measure the dog's rate of salivation. Soon the dog was salivating when it heard the bell —even before the food appeared. Salivation is, of course, a natural response to the taste or smell of food. But now Pavlov had conditioned the dog to salivate even when food was not present—it was, Pavlov said, a conditioned response.

Pavlov also discovered that the dog could unlearn the conditioned response. If the bell was rung and no food followed, the dog tired of the exercise and stopped salivating. With such experiments Pavlov proved that conditioned habits or responses could be extinguished as well as created.

It was evident from Pavlov's experiments that there are four different stages or elements in the conditioning process. First, the process was started by the dog's hunger, his natural drive to eat. Then there was the stimulus of the bell that provoked the response of premature salivation. Finally, the dog's response was rewarded or reinforced—he was fed. Conditioning, then, followed a drive-stimulus-response-reinforcement cycle. It was immediately plain that this sequence could be observed operating in the world of human learning.

Pavlov's canine experiments fired the imagination of the scientific world, especially that of psychologists in the United States, where much of the research on conditioning has been done. Three pioneers in this work have been John B. Watson, Edward L. Thorndike and B. F. Skinner. All three extended and refined the work of Pavlov, further examining how forces

Instilling a fear of Santa Claus

The psychologist John B. Watson pioneered conditioned learning in the U.S. Watson's extreme view, which shocked his contemporaries during the 1920s, held that human beings were little more than automatons shaped by conditioning forces in the environment.

Even more shocking than his view, to many people, was the experiment in which Watson demonstrated the idea on an 11-month-old child. First he showed the child, Albert, a succession of furry animals; the child exhibited no fear.

Then an assistant struck a steel bar with a hammer each time Albert saw an animal. The baby quickly associated the frightening noise with all furry objects.

Watson held that though the capacity to become frightened is innate, the association of fear with specific objects must be learned. The experiment was repeated on other children and recorded on film. Still photographs were made from the film and were heavily retouched. Copies of these pictures are reproduced below.

In Watson's experiment an eight-month-old baby who is not afraid of furry animals is presented with a large rabbit. The child pats the animal and exhibits natural curiosity but no fear.

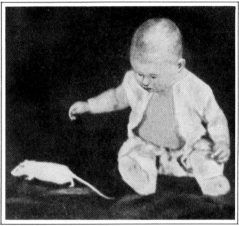

The same baby is shown a white rat for the first time. Although the animal would startle many adults, the child displays no fright. Watson believed this observation indicated fear was not inherited.

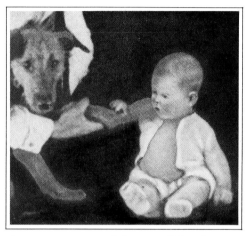

A more extreme test of the unconditioned child occurs when an Airedale, much larger than the baby, is introduced. The child reaches out to touch the animal's paw but still is not disturbed.

But after the child has been conditioned to fear furry creatures—by striking a steel bar to make a loud noise when a rabbit is brought near—his behavior changes. The rabbit now frightens him.

Once conditioned to shy from furry animals, the child seeks to escape when a muff is put down in front of him. By now, he is terrified by dogs, cats, rabbits, rats and all furry or hairy objects.

So thoroughly has the child been taught to fear furry or hairy objects that even the sight of Santa Claus's beard frightens him. Watson later deconditioned this child to remove his fears.

visible in his experiments—drive, stimulus, response and reinforcement—affect the process of learning in animals and in man.

The implications of Pavlov's discoveries were first grasped by Watson, a South Carolina-born psychologist at the Johns Hopkins University in Baltimore. Watson was a gruff, hearty man with single-minded enthusiasms, and his enthusiasm for Pavlovian theory was unrestrained. He loudly proclaimed not only that Pavlov's theories were correct but also that they explained virtually all human behavior. Man, to Watson, was little more than a stimulus-response machine; such humanistic notions as love and desire, he insisted, are really only manifestations of conditioned glandular or muscular responses in the body. Human behavior, in Watson's mechanistic view, was simply a succession of physical responses to stimuli coming from the environment.

Watson made a famous and somewhat bloodcurdling boast concerning the omnipotence of conditioning: "Give me a dozen healthy infants, well formed, and my own specified world to bring them up in, and I'll guarantee to take anyone at random and train him to become any type of specialist I might select—doctor, lawyer, artist, merchant-chief, and yes, even beggarman and thief, regardless of his talents, penchants, tendencies, abilities, vocations, and the race of his ancestors." In fairness to Watson, it should be added that he envisioned conditioning as a benign force to be used to improve education, especially that of children coming from disadvantaged racial and ethnic groups, thus affording all people an equal chance in life. Watson hoped to stamp out forever any notion that one racial inheritance is superior to any other.

One of Watson's most famous experiments involved an 11-month-old child named Albert. Watson, aided by a laboratory assistant named Rosalie Rayner, placed a furry white rat in a room with Albert. As the child reached out to pet the animal, Watson made a loud noise, striking a steel bar with a hammer and frightening the child. This action was repeated until the noise and the rat were paired in Albert's mind and he could no longer see a rat without crying and screaming in terror. Watson also discovered that conditioning had caused Albert to be terrified by anything soft, white and furry, including a rabbit, cotton wool, fur coats, white hair and even the white beard on a Santa Claus mask. Psychologists now call this "stimulus generalization"—that is, a process in which similar stimuli evoke the same response.

Watson has remained a controversial figure in the history of psychology, largely because of his extreme view of man-as-machine. People have also been distressed at the methods Watson used to condition Albert—and also at the thought that Watson never removed the child's terrors of white fur: Albert was taken home from the hospital where Watson performed the experiment before his fears could be deconditioned. (Watson somewhat lamely excused himself on the grounds that had Albert not come to the hospital he would nevertheless have picked up some comparable fear at home.) In later experiments Watson was careful to remove the fears he

A crude box, made from an old crate for bean cans, was used by psychologist Edward Thorndike to show that animals learn by stimulus-response conditioning. Thorndike put a cat in the box and set outside some food that the cat could reach only by pulling a latch string. Stimulated by the food, the cat learned through trial and error the correct response of pulling the string to open the door.

The controversial psychologist B. F. Skinner taught pigeons to walk figure 8s, play a kind of table tennis and even operate guided-missile control panels by conditioning them with rewards of grain for every correct move. Skinner, who coined the phrase operant conditioning to describe his method of training animals, concluded that all human behavior can similarly be controlled by reinforcements and rewards.

created in other children. Having made these later subjects afraid of white, furry animals by his usual method, Watson would stop clanging his steel bar and slowly reintroduce the animals under soothing conditions—during mealtime, for instance. The children would forget their fear and develop new associations between the animals and pleasure.

These famous experiments opened a pathway for psychotherapy that has only recently been widely exploited. Much neurotic behavior is learned through conditioning. People suffering from neuroses have accidentally been conditioned to make their irrational responses—perhaps through unwise handling in early childhood—in much the same fashion that Albert and the other children were taught their fear of the white rat and Santa's beard. Watson showed how it was possible to decondition the children, extinguishing their fear of the animals, and psychotherapists have found they can use a similar deconditioning process to help extinguish their patients' other phobias or neurotic behavior.

Watson has remained controversial, however, partly because of a popular guide to child upbringing that he wrote for parents: he recommended that mothers cultivate greater independence in the young by showing as little love for their children as possible. A kiss on the forehead at bedtime and a handshake at breakfast were, he said, affection enough for the day. Watson later repudiated this chilling volume, but probably not before its recommendations had blighted a number of childhoods. His scientific work was cut short when, in 1920, he divorced his wife and married his assistant, Rosalie Rayner. The divorce scandalized many members of the Johns Hopkins faculty and the board of trustees (conditioned, Watson doubtlessly would have said, to regard marriage as sacrosanct) and he was asked for his resignation. Watson subsequently enjoyed a second ca-

A crash course for canines

A tweedy English woman named Barbara Woodhouse has applied the principles of operant conditioning to dog training so effectively that she can turn an unruly mutt into an obedient pet in six and a half hours. Over the years, she has taught more than 14,500 dogs through a system that emphasizes reinforcements and rewards.

Mrs. Woodhouse utilizes a combination of voice commands, arm signals and abrupt jerks on a leash with a choke chain collar, which locks and clicks but does not hurt the dog. Every correct response is rewarded by praise and hugs. This system is so effective that Mrs. Woodhouse says she can train a dog to lie, sit or heel in five minutes.

It is teaching the dog owners to handle their pets properly that takes time. "I will not hear a word against the dogs," she says to owners who make mistakes. "There's nothing wrong with the dogs; it's all your fault."

As a new class gets underway, Mrs. Woodhouse supervises the leashing of the pets. While the animals are being readied, she explains that every command should be prefaced with the name of the dog: "Fido, sit," or "Fifi, heel."

To make a dog lie down (left), Mrs. Woodhouse applies pressure on the leash with her foot, causing the collar to make a noise that emphasizes her command.

Lavish affection and praise are the reinforcement and reward for the dog that has executed a command correctly (above). "I automatically feel friends with dogs," Mrs. Woodhouse says. "I hope I sound loving as well as firm."

Toward the end of a training session, Mrs. Woodhouse demonstrates her mastery over the dogs by commanding them to lie down. Untrained at the start of the session, the dogs will remain flattened until she gives another command.

reer as an advertising executive, successfully using aspects of psychological theory to analyze consumer responses.

One of the questions Watson failed to answer was why some responses prevail over others and why some eventually die out. It was a contemporary of Watson, Edward L. Thorndike, who recognized the vital importance of repetition and reward. Thorndike proposed that the unsuccessful response is weakened by its own lack of success and tends to fade out, while the correct response is strengthened by its own success.

In the history of psychology, Thorndike is as famous for his cats as Pavlov is for his dogs. He rounded up cats by the score from the alleys of New York and took them to his flat in an old rooming house. There he constructed makeshift cages out of old packing boxes. Each cage was fitted with a latch that could be opened from the inside by the hungry cat if the cat pulled a string. Outside the cage was a tempting bowl of food. The problem for the cat, of course, was to find the string and give it a yank with a

claw. Initially it took each of the cats a long period of trial and error to discover the string, pull it and release the latch. But, Thorndike discovered, once a cat had learned the proper solution, it took the animal less time to pull the string on a subsequent trial, still less time on a third try and so on. Clearly a successful response was strengthened by its own success while unsuccessful responses died out.

Thorndike's discoveries with animals went significantly beyond the findings of Pavlov. They showed that animals could do more than merely respond to stimuli by salivating. Their behavior could be shaped by reinforcements. Thorndike's cats could learn to do things that had positive outcomes, to solve problems, to operate on the world around them.

Through a long and busy teaching career at Columbia—Thorndike wrote or co-authored more than 500 books and articles—he continued his animal experiments and also extended his findings to human learning. Among other things, he helped to cause a minor revolution in the treatment of children at home and in the school. It was long thought that punishment was a natural and necessary part of child upbringing—"spare the rod and spoil the child" was accepted dogma. Thorndike demonstrated that punishment in the classroom or in the home could become counterproductive. Punishing a child for not learning his lessons or for failing to perform chores around the house does not necessarily spur the child to greater efforts, Thorndike found, but may stifle any desire for improvement. A reward for good performance, he maintained, even if only a few words of praise, is far more effective, not to mention more humane.

Thorndike's experiments with cats led to the far more complex behavior-shaping work of Burrhus Frederic Skinner, the much publicized Harvard psychology professor who has proclaimed that mankind's only hope is to condition all men to be peace-loving and cooperative. By systematic uses of reward, Skinner conditioned his own experimental animals, mostly pigeons and rats, to do all manner of things—one pair of pigeons learned to play a kind of table-tennis game with their beaks. Pavlov's techniques, which did not teach dogs new tricks but only involved the animals' built-in reflexes, have come to be called "classical conditioning." Skinner coined the phrase "operant conditioning" to indicate that he, like Thorndike, taught his animals to operate—to act—on their environment. They learned what to do and when to do it.

Skinner's principal tool has been the so-called Skinner box, a shiny, efficient version of Thorndike's patched-together cat boxes. The Skinner box provides the animal with freedom to wander around and to respond at will to levers or push buttons inside while its responses are recorded. Skinner's pigeons soon discovered that pecking one of the push buttons (called response keys) brought a reward, such as a bit of birdseed. The food was dispensed, however, only if the animal was following the pattern of behavior Skinner wanted it to learn. Once it had learned which behavior was rewarded, it could be stimulated to repeat that behavior over and over again. Then Skinner could proceed to teach it still another behavior pattern, link-

Toilet training, as practiced by this German mother and her child, is an example of learning by conditioning, in which a child is conditioned to control her immediate bodily needs and change her behavior by the reinforcement of the mother's praise and attention.

ing response after response until the bird could perform such complex tricks as playing Ping-Pong.

Skinner's great contribution was the discovery that conditioning could proceed in small steps. Animals could be taught very complicated behavior, he found, if rewards were given before total success was achieved. The desired behavior was broken down into many stages, and each stage leading toward success was rewarded. Gradually, as each stage was stimulated and rewarded, the individual stages combined into the ultimate behavior. To teach a pigeon to nudge a ball into a hole in the front left corner of its box, for example, a reward might first be given whenever the pigeon moved the ball forward, but withheld whenever the ball moved backward. Once the pigeon had learned to move the ball forward consistently, the reward was then dispensed only if the ball moved both forward and leftward. Finally, the reward would be withheld unless the ball dropped into the hole.

Skinner has always been quick to attempt practical applications of his operant-conditioning techniques. One of the most remarkable was a deadly serious project undertaken with government support during World War II: he set out to train pigeons to serve as kamikaze pilots inside a crude type of guided missile. The missile was a big bomb with a primitive steering mechanism controlled by a pigeon in its nose cone. Skinner trained a pigeon to peck at the center of a picture of an enemy ship that appeared on a screen. An electrode attached to the pigeon's beak activated an electronic circuit that could be used to correct the direction of the missile, and the bird's pecking would keep the missile aimed toward the target. Outlandish though the idea seems, it worked, at least in the laboratory. The pigeons never saw action, however, for other, more easily managed guidance mechanisms were developed.

Skinner's most important research was completed during the 1940s and 1950s. Since then a number of scientists have added further refinements to the knowledge of conditioning. They have shown that heredity—innate behavior patterns evolved over thousands and millions of years—has a powerful effect on what is learned and how it is learned. Some of this additional information has come from observation of the way human beings act, but much of it, as in the past, has been drawn from studies of the behavior of animals.

Keller and Marian Breland, proprietors of Animal Behavorial Enterprises in Arkansas (an organization that supplies trained animals for zoos and shows), discovered that ancient ingrained habits interfered with their attempts to teach tricks to animals. They tried to train a raccoon to pick up two coins with its paws and to drop them into a box. Although the Brelands carefully followed established procedures of conditioning and pursued all the techniques of reward and punishment, they discovered that instead of dropping the coins in the box the animal started to rub them together in miserly fashion. The harder the trainers worked, the more pronounced this unexpected activity became. The Brelands concluded that

Mass conditioning in Nazi Germany in the 1930s culminated in gigantic rallies, where party leaders played on Pavlovian responses to elicit adulation from seething mobs. Here, in Berlin in 1938, the passing of Führer Adolf Hitler's motorcade provokes a collective conditioned reflex of upthrust arms and chants.

the animal was exhibiting "washing behavior"—an instinct evolved by the raccoon's ancestors eons ago for removing the exoskeleton of a crayfish, one of the creature's favorite dishes. Further, the raccoon seemed to be exhibiting Pavlovian classical conditioning. The coins had become linked in its brain with its reward of food and it insisted on treating the coins as if they too were food.

The raccoon's behavior points to a principle of conditioning first detected by Thorndike decades before: stimulus and reward procedures must not contradict natural reflexes or instincts. Pigeons naturally peck for food, and they readily learn to peck the push buttons in Skinner boxes for the same reward. An action naturally alien to the reward cannot be taught. Thorndike had earlier found that his cats could not be conditioned to gain escape from their boxes by yawning or licking themselves. Instead the cats insisted on using their natural complement of weapons and tools—their claws and teeth. Of course cats do yawn and they spend hours grooming their fur. But these actions, having nothing to do with the cats' ingrained methods of defense and escape, could not be hooked up, so to speak, to accomplish their release from the boxes.

That such built-in wiring of inherited behaviors also regulates human learning was demonstrated by Martin E. P. Seligman of the University of Pennsylvania, who discovered from personal experience what he calls the *sauce béarnaise* phenomenon. At a pre-opera dinner party, Seligman and his wife dined on filet mignon with *sauce béarnaise,* a favorite dish. Six hours later Seligman became violently ill with stomach flu. The next time he ordered what had been his favorite sauce, he could not bear the taste. Seligman concluded that he had become the victim of classical conditioning as far as the sauce was concerned. He was grateful, although somewhat puzzled as a scientist, that his conditioned revulsion did not also attach itself to dinner tables, plates, the opera or his wife. The reason, Seligman concluded, was the dependence of conditioning on a meaningful, natural set of associations—in this case the connection between taste and stomach illness. Even though his wife was present when he ate the sauce, she was not psychologically linked to the illness.

Seligman then noted another curious fact about the *sauce béarnaise* phenomenon; Pavlovian learning in the form of his new distaste for *sauce béarnaise* took place when the reinforcement—the punishment of illness—occurred hours after the response of eating. Normally such feedback, either reward or punishment, must follow rather quickly after a behavior occurs for reinforcement to take place. It appears that as far as the taste of food and stomach illness are concerned, human beings are wired to learn conditioned responses even after a lapse of several hours.

There are other blocks to the learning process. Two early psychological experimenters, Robert Yerkes and John D. Dodson, discovered that an animal will learn a behavior quickly when reinforced by a mild electrical shock, but that heavier shocks inhibit rather than quicken the learning process. The same kind of overkill has now been found to affect human learning. If the motivation to solve a problem is too high, it can make the solution harder to find rather than easier. Sam Glucksberg of Princeton's psychology department demonstrated this phenomenon by giving a number of student-subjects a problem to solve; some were promised a small reward for success, but others were offered a $20 prize. The students working for the small reward were distinctly the more successful. The subjects coveting the $20 prize tried to work too fast and too hard, in their eagerness repeating solutions already proved unsuccessful. Glucksberg confirmed Yerkes and Dodson in their conclusion that for any given task there is an optimum level of motivation, neither too low nor too high.

The principles of conditioning, which demonstrate how drive, stimulus, response and reward operate, have been worked out largely in laboratory experiments with animals. But they have very practical results. For one thing, they explain the process behind many kinds of human learning that were long assumed to be instinctive.

The role of a teacher in developing skills becomes clearer when his efforts are related to operant conditioning. The person learning golf or skiing or tennis—or how to run a drill press—acquires his skill as the correct muscular responses are rewarded by success and are therefore reinforced until they become habit. But there are hundreds of ways to hit a golf ball incorrectly, and only a few ways to do it correctly. An instructor helps the learner find the correct ways quickly, rather than through a long process of trial and error. Then with practice the learner can reinforce the correct muscular responses. There is a further reason, also related to conditioning, why early instruction is helpful. Left to himself, the neophyte golfer may discover a swing that sometimes knocks the ball a respectable distance down the fairway but that is nevertheless awkward and lacks consistency and power. However, since it is rewarded with at least occasional success, this bad swing becomes reinforced, dooming the player to repeat it. He remains a second-rate golfer unless laborious later instruction manages to extinguish the only partially successful muscular responses and substitute better ones.

Just as the knowledge of conditioning illuminates the way people learn skills, it reveals the origins of some of the most basic aspects of human behavior. Some characteristics that seem to be inherent turn out to be the result of learning. The drive to succeed, to move up in life, so marked in advanced, industrialized societies, is a learned drive. Two longtime Yale University psychologists, John Dollard and Neal E. Miller, suggest that this drive is implanted by the way children are brought up. Parents and schoolteachers in most advanced cultures constantly urge children to hurry and grow up, to learn new skills quickly, to improve. A backslider is made to feel guilty by being admonished not to "act like a baby." At each stage of growing up the child receives rewards for achievement—but the goal of further improvement is always held out in front of him like a carrot on a stick. Thus there is constant pressure, born both of fear of

Conditioning by practice, with a mirror to reinforce correct motions, enables a dancer to respond to the demands of his art.

punishment and hope for reward, to progress yet another step forward. This anxiety subsequently pervades adult behavior and provides a powerful drive to get ahead in the world.

Another unspoken, taken-for-granted Western drive, perhaps even more fundamental than the motivation to succeed, is the urge to think and talk logically. This also, according to Miller and Dollard, is learned behavior, deeply implanted in childhood. Many parents insist that even a quite young child coherently explain what he has been doing (or planning to do) and tend to be severe when contradictions and absurdities creep into the narrative. Punished by parents' displeasure when his explanations are illogical, the child develops an anxiety-fueled drive to be rational. And this remains a lifelong, deeply implanted attitude. That the needs to be logical and to get ahead are not inborn is suggested by the fact that they are neither universal nor immutable. They are more emphasized in Western Europe, for example, than in India.

Most psychologists study conditioning in order to learn more about the way people learn. They look upon it as a process that helps analyze behavior. But conditioning is also a tool, a method of helping people to learn in a practical way. Its principles have been used unconsciously for millennia by teachers, parents and animal trainers. The discoveries of this century have enabled them to be applied in refined and very direct ways. This process of deliberate application of conditioning techniques began even before Skinner attempted to train pigeons as missile controllers, but in recent years it has accelerated greatly.

Conditioning techniques are now widely put to work to teach people new kinds of behavior. Systems of reward are employed, for example, in a number of mental hospitals to encourage the patients to break the destructive behavior patterns caused by their illnesses and to take part in more normal activities. Systems of reward have also been used effectively in schools for retarded children. If the retarded child successfully performs a task assigned him by the teacher, he receives a piece of candy, perhaps, or a symbolic reward such as a poker chip that he can trade in for a piece of candy at lunchtime. The reward reinforces the desired behavior, helping to teach the retarded child to perform tasks he probably could not learn in any other way.

Systems of punishment, on the other hand, have been used to help adults break harmful habits. The punishments employed in what psychologists call aversion therapy are not severe—a mild electric shock at worst—but they are annoying and become paired in the patient's mind with the habit he is trying to conquer. A problem drinker, for instance, seeking help in a clinic, might have an electrode attached to the back of his hand. If he reaches for a bottle, the clinician overseeing the project gives him a mild shock through the electrode. Repeated over and over, such a procedure conditions the drinker to associate alcohol with pain and may help him kick the habit. Similar techniques have been used to help addicts give up drugs and smokers to give up cigarettes.

In a triumph of conditioned learning, Danish gymnasts execute a perfectly coordinated "jump jack" flying leap. All the elements of operant conditioning combine in the mass precision of this difficult maneuver: innate aptitudes, the refinement of years of practice and teaching, and reinforcement at every stage by the rewards of success.

Conditioning specialists believe that individuals can learn to condition themselves through these same principles of punishments or rewards. Skinner and his colleagues described in the introduction to one of their technical handbooks how they conditioned themselves to get through the difficult and often tiresome task of completing the book. One successful trick, they discovered, was to provide themselves a room where they did nothing but write, no matter whether for eight minutes or eight hours. After a period of time the room became associated with writing and their work on the book proceeded more rapidly. Psychologist Logan J. Fox, working with students with poor study habits, suggested that each student always go to a single place to study, remove all distracting objects and leave the place immediately when he found his mind beginning to stray. Fox reported that the study habits of the group improved markedly.

Perhaps the most widespread use of conditioning techniques as a teaching tool is not, oddly, in formal education but in advertising. An advertisement is meant to teach its audience to buy something—an object, a service, an idea—and to choose that product in preference to others that may be very similar. In many cases today the ad attempts to achieve this by conditioning—the calculated use of a stimulus that invokes a common human drive and promises a reward through purchase of the advertised product. Often the reward is a release from, or lessening of, an unpleasant drive such as fear. One soft-drink company for years appealed to the fear, especially strong among adolescents, of not belonging, of being lonely, of being unaccepted by the group. The advertisements stressed togetherness, reproducing pictures of young people grouped around a campfire or resting together after a hike—and always satisfying their thirst by drinking the company's product.

Many other successful advertising campaigns are based on similar offers of reduction in the consumer's uncomfortable drives of anxiety and fear. But some take the opposite tack, offering a reward of felicity if the product is used. The people pictured in such advertisements are generally youthful, vigorous and good-looking, as if these desirable qualities were somehow magically produced by purchasing the right product. The humorist S. J. Perelman once noted that, in ladies' underwear advertisements employing the before-and-after technique, the "before" picture portrayed a tired model in tacky surroundings. In the "after" picture, however, the purchase of the right kind of new girdle had not only made the model's figure more lissome, but also seemed somehow to have improved her hairdo, erased the crow's feet from around her eyes, reupholstered the divan and repapered the walls.

The most ambitious scheme for applying conditioning techniques to practical and beneficent ends has been advanced by Skinner. In his didactic novel *Walden Two* and the philosophical tract *Beyond Freedom and Dignity*, he has proposed the startling idea of reshaping man and his culture through conditioning. He believes it is possible to teach everyone to act in socially desirable ways and to avoid socially undesirable behavior. Skinner points out that people are already being conditioned—by family, school and friends—to adopt certain patterns of life. Too often this conditioning seems to produce not benevolent and useful behavior, but rather its opposite—aggression, belligerence, covetousness. Why not, Skinner asks, establish systematic teaching programs that will condition all men from childhood on to be peaceful and productive, with all destructive and wasteful emotions "trained out"?

A character in *Walden Two*, Frazier, who often seems to speak for Skinner, explains that "the productive and strengthening emotions—joy and love" will be reinforced by systems of rewards from early childhood on. "But sorrow and hate—and the high-voltage excitements of anger, fear and rage—are out of proportion with the needs of modern life, and they're wasteful and dangerous." So they will be systematically eliminated by conditioned learning. In the community of Twin Oaks in Virginia, whose members are trying to put into practice Skinner's concepts of social engineering, a member who becomes angry or aggressive is simply ignored —there is no reinforcement of any kind. Members showing cooperative and affectionate behavior, on the other hand, are singled out for praise by the group, made to feel special and highly valued. In *Walden Two*, Frazier explains that it is through exactly such techniques that a human race cured of aggression, angers and the fear of isolation would be able to create a "social structure which will satisfy the needs of everyone and in which everyone will want to observe the supporting code."

Such a social structure, points out Castle, another character in *Walden Two*, implies a planned society with a dictator at the head of it. Frazier readily agrees. "But it's a limited sort of despotism. . . . And I don't think anyone should worry about it. The despot must wield his power for the good of others."

Many critics have echoed Castle's skepticism, for despots over the millennia have seldom been "philosopher kings" (to use Plato's phrase) selflessly and justly wielding their powers for others' good. Skinner's vision of utopia may have serious flaws. But Skinner seems to be amply justified in his faith that through positive conditioning—careful, kindly training employing rewards but never punishment—mankind could be made wiser and happier. For the power and usefulness of this process of learning are now established beyond question.

The well-conditioned consumer

Perhaps the most spectacular—and successful—use of modern understanding of learning is in advertising. It entices people into learning things they did not know they wanted to learn—to prefer one product over another similar product. It does this, in many instances, by applying the stimulus and response mechanism of classic conditioning.

The key to the advertisers' method is the employment of props and settings that people have been conditioned to associate with status, success, adventure or sensual gratification. A maker of mentholated cigarettes may display his product with an iced drink *(page 57)* or against a background of a rippling stream and a sylvan glade, because he knows people learned from childhood experience that such a setting is cool and fresh. Its image in a picture is enough to stimulate thoughts of these qualities and, the advertiser hopes, to generate the response of a purchase.

Each of the advertisements at the right and on the following pages is an example of this kind of calculated appeal. Each has been carefully contrived to capitalize on some well-conditioned attitude. All this effort is expended because the advertiser knows that his product—whether a package of cigarettes, a pair of shoes or a bubble bath—is competing against thousands of others and must have something special to attract buyers.

When an advertisement manages to capitalize on the customer's conditioning effectively, the response becomes an automatic reflex. People think of the product in a special way without realizing it. When that happens, they often do something else the advertiser wants them to do—they buy the product.

This 1957 advertisement shows more than a dashing convertible. To many Americans, who have been conditioned by movies, TV and even by school textbooks to equate the life style represented here with succeeding, the house, the tree-shaded lawn—and the auto itself—spell status.

Roßkastanien-Extrakt, Vitamine,
Chlorophyll, Lanolin und andere Naturöle.
Erst diese einzigartige Komposition
natürlicher Wirkstoffe macht dieses
Schaumbad zu dem, was es ist:
badedas.

badedas duftet natürlich natürlich.

A pair of cool appeals to the senses

"Badedas smells natural naturally," says a German message for bubble bath. And the explicit promise of the slogan is underscored with a stimulus recalling a natural source of refreshment.

To suggest the soothing taste of this mentholated French cigarette, the advertiser decorated the package with crème de menthe on the rocks ("bien frappée" in French), thereby stimulating both the eye and the palate.

Bien frappée !

ROYALE
MENTHOL

Companionable drink: the key to belonging

Visions of a glittering beach and adventures shared by a gorgeous girl and a good-looking man are familiar stimulants to thoughts of romance. A part of that scene, says this advertiser, is a picnic including his brand of vodka.

Full of vitality and a sense of shared fun, these French models are fulfilling the deeply held need to be a part of the group. The key to belonging, says the advertiser, is the soft drink that brings together young people who have "a thirst for life, a thirst for truth."

Soif d'aujourd'hui,
c'est la soif de vivre, la soif du vrai.
Coca-Cola, par exemple.
Pourquoi accepter moins?

Soif d'aujourd'hui

59

A virile man, an elegant woman

Marlboro. Der Geschmack von Freiheit und Abenteuer.

Hol' Dir diesen vollen Geschmack. **Marlboro**

Movies, television, books and magazines have conditioned people the world over to regard the weatherworn face and ten-gallon hat of the American cowboy as a symbol of masculinity. The message is simple: this cigarette is for he-men— "the flavor of freedom and adventure."

In the fashion world, the name of couturier Yves St. Laurent evokes a special response. The advertiser of the cigarettes displayed here is taking advantage of the fact that women all over the world have been conditioned by fashion magazines to associate that name with elegance and sophistication.

Shoes by Yves St. Laurent. Cigarettes by John Player.

The Conceptual World

3

Comedian Mort Sahl once told a joke about a bank robber who passed a note to a frightened teller behind the cage. The note read: "This is a stick-up. Act normal."

Promptly the teller responded: "What's normal?"

Sahl's anecdote is something more than just a joke. It revolves around what is called a concept—the idea of normality. Concepts can be simple and can refer to concrete everyday things. Chair is a concept. There are millions of chairs in the world of every conceivable shape from plastic bubbles to Louis XIV antiques, but they are all chairs, nonetheless. Included in the concept are all pieces of furniture whose primary purpose is to provide a place for people to sit down. Woman is also a relatively straightforward concept, although it includes females of many sizes, ages and shapes.

But there are abstract concepts that are notorious for their complexity and their tendency to start arguments: justice, freedom, education, learning itself. As the Mort Sahl story implies, normality is one of these complex concepts. It is a large umbrella under which are gathered many notions of acceptable and expectable behavior. The concept differs widely from one person to another. A man whose experience of the world is limited might have a very narrow concept of what is normal—behavior pretty much like his own. An anthropologist, on the other hand, who has studied behavior in many different cultures, might have a broader concept: normal behavior to him may include anything that is consistent with the culture in which the individual grows up. The psychiatrist, who is exposed to strange forms of behavior among his patients, may have an even broader and more elusive view of normality.

Whether concepts are complex or simple, they are essential to human learning. Anyone who had never learned the concept of chair would be baffled each time he saw such a piece of furniture; he would be forced to rediscover repeatedly what it was intended for. More complex concepts, even though hard to define, are also essential. Without some concept of justice, for example, civilization would be impossible.

Concepts enable people to grasp the main resemblances between things and to ignore irrelevant details, to move from the concrete to the abstract, from single to multiple, and from the whole to a part and again to the whole. Thus concept learning is essential to the organization, flexibility and progress of thought. An understanding of the role of concepts helps show how people think, how they use their brains to solve ordinary everyday problems like measuring a piece of wood and extraordinary problems like deducing the nature and operation of atomic particles too small to be seen.

Concept learning runs in tandem with and complements conditioned learning. The classical conditioning described by Pavlov (*Chapter 2*) teaches humans what to expect of the world and how to respond to it: the child who is burned by a hot radiator almost reflexively draws his hand away from steaming radiators ever after. Operant conditioning tells the child, or adult, how to behave to receive desired rewards; the tennis enthusiast must practice the proper stroke over and over to win the reward of playing tennis well.

Concept learning operates in a different way. It teaches people how to think about the world around them, how to organize experience and begin to understand it. The ability to create concepts, says psychologist Jerome Bruner of Oxford, "saves us from being overwhelmed by the complexity of our society, for if we had to respond to each stimulus separately we would be unable to adjust."

The process of learning concepts begins early in life. It is a critical part of children's mental development. Seeing how they acquire concepts as they grow is perhaps the clearest way to perceive how concepts in general are formed and understood. For example, a child growing up in a green leafy suburb becomes accustomed at an early age to seeing robins and wrens and other common birds flying past the house, pecking for food on the lawn or visiting a feeding station. The child learns even before he begins to use language that these curious flying creatures resemble one another, that is, they have properties in common. They hop about and always fly away if he tries to come near them. When the child develops language ability, he discovers that there is a label, "birds," that covers this general class of flying creatures. He thus learns a concept that unites and organizes everything with feathers.

As the child grows, his ability to perceive concepts, refine them and relate them improves. Thus, when the youngster who has based his concept of birds on robins is taken to the zoo, his concept undergoes a sudden change. He sees a pelican, penguins, an ostrich. The ostrich may weigh 300 pounds, perhaps 2,000 times as much as a robin, and it does not fly. Neither do the penguins, which waddle instead with comic, lurching sedateness. The pelican flies, but that is the end of its resemblance to a robin. The child is forced to change his concept of birds to include a far larger assortment of creatures. It is this ability to modify and enlarge concepts—making them broader, more inclusive, more accurate reflections of reality—that constitutes intellectual growth or learning.

Investigations of the way the mind forms concepts go back to the Greeks. Aristotle discerned a fundamental truth about the process when he suggested that human intelligence must include a capacity for abstract thinking. The sense organs, he noted, cannot perceive universal ideas or categories; they merely pick up impressions of the things they touch, see, hear, smell, feel. Therefore, Aristotle said, it must be a power inherent in the mind that sorts these impressions into concepts.

Aristotle's theory that the mind forms concepts from the data the senses present to it has been exhaustively documented in this century by the most brilliant and painstaking student of conceptual learning in children, the Swiss psychologist Jean Piaget. Although not widely known outside psychological and scholastic circles, Piaget is rated by some authorities as one of the most important psychological investigators of this century. "After Freud," says Harvard psychologist Roger Brown, "it is Jean Piaget, I think, who has made the greatest contribution to modern psychology."

Piaget, a rumpled, tweedy figure with horn-rimmed glasses—in his later years he looked like everyone's idea of a wise grandfather—began his lifelong study of children in the 1920s by observing his own son and two daughters. Many psychologists of the time tended to dismiss his work on the grounds that such seemingly casual observations could not be trusted. But Piaget was a wonderfully accurate and sensitive observer and was endlessly inventive in devising for his children little tasks that illuminated their stages of mental development. His reports of his home experiments present charming pictures of childhood. On one occasion Piaget placed his watch chain, an object that fascinated his daughter Lucienne, in a matchbox, leaving the box partly open. Lucienne, then 16 months old, studied the situation for a moment, then opened her mouth wide. Having rehearsed the solution to the problem with her mouth, she then quickly opened the matchbox and secured the coveted chain.

On another occasion Piaget was experimenting to test the inventiveness of his other daughter, Jacqueline, who was only one year old at the time. It was Piaget's watch, rather than the watch chain, that fascinated Jacqueline. So Piaget put the watch on the floor near Jacqueline's playpen just beyond her reach and laid the chain along the floor in her direction. He then hid part of the chain by placing a small cushion over it. As Piaget recorded in his notes: "Jacqueline at first tries to grasp the watch directly. Not succeeding, she looks at the chain. She notes that the latter is under the cushion. Then Jacqueline removes the latter at one stroke and pulls the chain while looking at the watch." What intrigued Piaget, of course, was the fact that although the watch was beyond her reach, Jacqueline was inventive enough to see that she could succeed in getting hold of it by using an indirect means—pulling the chain.

After his own children were grown, Piaget continued his experimental work, studying hundreds of children who attended the Institut Jean-Jacques Rousseau, a branch of Geneva University that included a school for children and a research center dealing with child psychology. His findings about the development of concept learning were reported in some 30 books and more than 150 articles.

Copernicus' concept of the solar system, illustrated here in a 17th Century drawing, placed the sun rather than the earth at the center, with the planets revolving around it. This doctrine reordered man's view of the universe.

Ideas that shook the world

Every so often the human mind generates a revolutionary idea. It may be Charles Darwin's theory that man has evolved from apelike ancestors. It may be the discovery by the French microbiologist Louis Pasteur that diseases are transmitted by germs. When such a dynamic concept occurs, the world is never quite the same again.

On these pages four revolutionary concepts are represented. They come from widely different fields: astronomy, art, religion and politics. But they share an important attribute: each of them shook the world.

Martin Luther's challenge to the authority of the Catholic Church, signaled by the nailing of his theses to the door of the Church of All Saints in Wittenberg, led to the Protestant Reformation, splitting Christianity.

Pablo Picasso's dynamic painting Les Demoiselles d'Avignon drew hostile reactions from critics but marked a new approach to art in the 20th Century.

Nikolai Lenin's advocacy of the concept of the revolution of the proletariat, which he expounded at Finland Station in Petrograd in 1917, triggered the overthrow of the Russian government and, ultimately, the spread of Communism throughout a large part of the world.

Piaget's studies convinced him that children learn to form concepts and develop intellectually in a sequence of four principal stages. All children go through the same stages and in the same order, although some may move faster than others. Apparently the child's growing brain develops the ability to make certain intellectual connections only in a fixed sequence based on age and experience.

The first of these stages lasts until the child is 18 months to two years old. Piaget has called this the period of "sensorimotor intelligence"; the child learns largely through physical contact with his surroundings—sucking and handling his toys and other objects. In the second period, between the ages of two and seven, the child learns language, which vastly expands his ability to learn concepts, because he can now label everything. But his logical powers are still feeble; the mind is simply not yet equipped to make certain sorts of connections. In Piaget's third period—seven years to 11—logical, problem-solving abilities grow swiftly. But the child still operates best in dealing with concrete objects—thus Piaget's name for this period, "concrete operational." In the final period, from age 11 onward, the mind is liberated from that need for the concrete; it becomes capable of handling abstract concepts, hypotheses, theories. The teenager develops that uniquely human ability to think about thought.

The four stages are, in a sense, cumulative: the child cannot progress to stage three, for example, until he has mastered the experiences of the second stage; one stage builds on another. But the four types of mind represented by these stages are quite different. It is as if the growing child were mentally four different people in succession, his mind at various periods comparable to four different models of computers ascending from the very simple to the very complex.

One of the most important steps in Piaget's first period of growth occurs when the child develops what Piaget calls "object constancy." Up to the age of six months or so the infant has no awareness that things exist even when he cannot see them. If a toy slips beneath the covers in the crib, he does not even look for it. As far as the child is concerned, the toy is not simply hidden but annihilated.

Piaget saw this with one of his own little daughters. He showed her a rattle, and she made appropriate noises and reached for it. But when he put it behind his back, she lost interest. Out of sight, out of mind. In fact, out of sight, out of existence.

Some months later Piaget offered the rattle again, then hid it behind his back. His daughter, realizing that the rattle still existed, started to reach behind Piaget's back. She had arrived at an important conceptual stage, the understanding that objects have an independent existence—object constancy—whether they are visible or not.

During this same stage of development, the infant makes at least some acquaintance with other basic concepts. He develops a rudimentary notion of cause and effect—if he pushes on a tower of blocks that he has built, the tower will tumble down. And he acquires a rudimentary understanding of

The pioneer Swiss psychologist Jean Piaget deduced the basic principles of human intellectual growth by closely observing the development of thought processes and learning patterns in his own children from infancy through the years of childhood and adolescence.

space and time. He learns to locate his toys and he knows that the period of time called the day is divided into subunits—breakfast time, morning play, lunchtime, afternoon and so on.

At about 18 months children begin the long process of mastering the language of their native country. Learning that things have names immensely speeds the conceptualizing process. The first words a child uses are almost invariably the names of things that he has been handling and playing with. "Dog," "shoe" and "ball" are generally among the earliest words spoken after "Mommy" and "Daddy." Significantly, a child almost never uses the word diaper—that is something his mother deals with. Action words also emerge at this time, the most frequently used including "broken" and "gone." In short, the first concepts the child understands are everyday objects in his own immediate world.

In Piaget's next stage of development, from about two years to seven, the child continues to explore the rich world of childhood with his sensorimotor apparatus—climbing, digging, throwing things. But now he commands an ever-increasing number of words and demands to know the name of everything. In short, he is busy digesting and labeling concepts. He concentrates at first on concrete objects—chair, glass, table, bed—but later he begins to grasp more complex concepts like heavier and warmer, fair and unfair.

Piaget notes that a key activity in these years is make-believe play. By imitating the behavior of adults, children learn to come to terms with the adult world around them. Often, for example, children come home after the first days of kindergarten and immediately start "playing school"; in this way they accustom themselves to such concepts as teacher and pupil and adjust to the new, unfamiliar school environment into which they have abruptly been thrust.

In these years, however, the child still is confused by many simple, but unfamiliar, concepts. He has noticed that everything that moves is alive —therefore he assumes the sun and moon are alive. He confuses the categories of natural and man-made. Natural things—stars, the sky, stones, trees—were created not by physical forces but by his parents, or perhaps by grandparents or other people who lived long ago. (Parents may be accorded such credit because they seem omniscient and omnipotent to the young child.) On the other hand, many things that an adult knows were created by humans, and can therefore be changed, are assumed by the five-year-old to be immutable. Piaget has quizzed children at this stage of development about playing marbles. Could the rules, he has asked, be changed? The four- or five-year-olds have almost invariably been shocked at the idea; the rules of marbles, they reply, have been fixed for all time and could not possibly be altered. Unless, of course, that omnipotent creature known as father decided the rules could be changed—then, just maybe, it would be all right.

Piaget devised a simple but instructive experiment to test the concept mastery of children at this stage in development. He took two stubby glass-

An 18-month-old girl, pressing her hands against a television set, is moving through what Swiss psychologist Jean Piaget called the sensorimotor stage of intellectual development. In this period, which starts at birth and lasts for about two years, the child learns by feeling and tasting, picking up, twisting, sucking and scrutinizing the objects around her.

es exactly the same size and filled them almost to the brim with milk or another familiar liquid such as lemonade. Then while a child watched he poured the milk or lemonade from one of the short glasses into a tall, skinny glass. Which glass, he then asked the child, held more liquid? Almost invariably the child said the tall, thin glass—the liquid in it was much higher. In like fashion Piaget rolled out a ball of soft clay into a long, thin snake. Which contained more clay, he asked, the ball or the snake? Children invariably chose the snake because it was longer.

It was evident from these experiments that kindergarten-age children understand the concepts of length and height, but not of volume or mass. They can comprehend only one dimension at a time—the tall glass's height but not its thinness. They also seem to ignore the notion of reversibility —that if the milk in the tall glass were poured back into the stubby one, the level, barring spillage, would be the same as it was when the experiment began. For some reason the child at this stage in his development cannot deal with such simple-seeming concepts. But Piaget discovered that children just a couple of years older—say seven or eight—have no trouble at all with these concepts. Asked whether the tall glass contains more milk or less, they will immediately answer "the same" with an implied "of course" in their tone of voice. They have mastered the concept Piaget calls the "constancy of volume," a critical step for the growing child striving to understand the world around him.

Some psychologists have demonstrated that children may reason better and sooner than Piaget has said. What holds them back from solving problems is sometimes faulty memory; the child cannot keep in mind all the elements of the problem to be solved. Five-year-olds, for example, when tested by a psychologist, may have trouble understanding this simple logical syllogism: if A is bigger than B and B is bigger than C, then A must be bigger than C. The young child cannot keep track of the ABCs, especially the difficult perception that B is two things at once—smaller than A but also bigger than C. However, young children can handle a comparable logical problem. When a five-year-old discovers that his mother and father are going out to supper, the child immediately asks, "Who's staying with me?" The logic involved is a syllogism that the child's mind can manage: "If my parents are going out, I will be alone. I am never alone. Therefore, a baby sitter must be coming to stay with me." Because the child is familiar with the facts that parents leave and baby sitters arrive, he readily remembers the parts of this logical proposition. Such observations may modify Piaget's timetable, but they do not invalidate his overall view that children develop conceptual abilities gradually and in a systematic order.

Piaget's view of the systematic progress of child development is borne out by a comparison between a five-year-old and a six-year-old. The five-year-old has trouble organizing things logically. The child's mind makes logical leaps; it cannot make sense out of the resemblances and common attributes among things. An experiment involving a five-year-old girl

A two-year-old, like this boy conversing with a policeman, has a vocabulary of around 150 words. He is just beginning to be able to express himself and communicate with others as he enters the stage of learning that Jean Piaget refers to as the preoperational period.

illustrates the difficulty. The child was a perfectly normal, bright little girl. She was given some red, blue and yellow triangles and squares and told to sort them out. First, she separated all the triangles and squares by colors, then she changed her mind and arranged them so that they were organized by shapes. Instead of putting a yellow triangle next to a yellow square, she put a red triangle next to a yellow triangle. But then, after she had made this arrangement, she moved the red triangle and put a blue one in its place. Evidently, at this stage, the child does not have a clear concept for organizing the triangles and squares; she moves impulsively from one arrangement to another.

Within a year or so this changes. A six-year-old can readily arrange things by their common attributes—and leave them that way. But at this stage the child has another kind of conceptual problem. The six-year-old cannot always keep straight the idea that the whole of something is always greater than any of its parts. If the child is shown a bowl of fruit containing five bananas, two apples and one orange, and is asked to name them, he will do so and he will probably be aware that they are all fruit.

A pair of uninhibited boys, pretending they are the popular television characters Batman and Robin, are engaged in what is known as symbolic play. In this part of Piaget's preoperational period of development, they begin to conceive of other people as entities that are entirely distinct from themselves.

But if the child is then asked whether there are more bananas than fruit in the bowl he will miss the correct answer. He will probably say that there are more bananas because he counts them and then compares them with the number of nonbananas, not remembering that the bananas, too, are fruit. For some reason the young child is unable to hold in his head the idea of whole and part at the same time.

Piaget has maintained that children cannot be hurried from one stage of development to another. Teachers have tried to train five-year-olds ·in constancy-of-volume observations; after a good deal of instruction the teachers have succeeded in getting the child to agree that the tall glass does not contain more milk than the stubby glass. But when the same amount of milk is poured into a large container, so that the liquid barely covers the bottom, the child is likely to say that now there is less, reverting to his earlier misconception. The conclusion Piaget draws from this is that the child's mind is not simply a small version of the adult mind, less trained and less informed. The child's mind is different, lacking some of the abilities that adults take for granted. Until the needed abilities are learned, the child cannot progress to the next level—and, Piaget implies, there is no use trying to speed the process.

In Piaget's third stage, roughly seven years to 11, the child's mind operates more logically—he easily sees that there will be the same amount of milk no matter how many times it is poured into different containers. At this stage in the timetable of learning the child also comprehends other concepts such as the conservation of mass (that there will be the same amount of clay whether it forms a ball or is rolled out flat) and conservation of weight (that a big package may be very light and weigh no more than a small but heavy package).

The child deals best with concrete things, actual objects or people he can count and handle, during this period, but he makes another big jump. He discovers how concepts are related, and how they combine to form larger categories. For example, he learns that the concepts of chair, couch and table can all be classed under the heading of furniture. The child also learns to reverse this process, breaking large concepts down into their components. He can think of the category furniture and call to mind tables and chairs, then lump them together again into such groups as bedroom furniture and living room furniture.

The fourth and last of Piaget's major stages of conceptual development covers roughly the teen-age years. The mind of the young person is now approaching the acuity—if not the experience and judgment—of the normal adult mind. A tremendous change has occurred. The teen-age intelligence can deal with abstract concepts; the mind is no longer tied to concrete things. The teenager can think about thought—can appreciate the importance of, say, parliamentary government, can appreciate the structure and themes (and not just the plot) of a novel, debate the nature of freedom, perform complex mathematical operations. A few years earlier, when he was only eight, he dealt in simple problems that were easily visualized in his mind—three pears and five apples make eight pieces of fruit. But now he can solve abstract problems in trigonometry, juggling relations among numbers, handling hypotheses and manipulating such mathematical concepts as angles, ratios and trigonometric functions.

The young person at this stage is constantly forming and revising concepts. Like the five-year-old who saw the strange feathered creatures at the zoo and was therefore forced to enlarge his concept of birds, the teenager finds information pouring in from everywhere—books, magazines, school, hobbies, conversation with parents and friends, personal observation of the world and its ways—forcing him to enlarge or refine his concepts and to manufacture many new ones.

Piaget believes that this enlarging and refining of the teenager's concepts —and, in fact, all concept learning from infancy to adulthood—involves two processes that he calls assimilation and accommodation. Assimilation is the process of adding a new piece of information to an already formed concept. The concept does not change radically, it merely expands to include the additional fact. Accommodation, on the other hand, involves remaking a concept to absorb many new pieces of information; the concept alters radically.

Suppose, for example, the child who forms his idea of birds from robins and wrens is told that the sparrow and the crow are also birds. The child would assimilate this information, enlarging but not otherwise changing his concept of birds. But then he goes to the zoo and sees penguins and ostriches. He is forced by the new evidence to alter his concept of bird to accommodate these un-birdlike creatures.

This sort of revising and refining of concepts goes on during all of Piaget's stages—if it did not, intellectual progress would cease. Very young children, for example, learn that some ways of playing games are fair and some are unfair. The concept of fairness broadens as the child assimilates many instances of fair and unfair behavior. Ultimately it will broaden and deepen until the teenager has worked out a sophisticated and abstract concept of justice.

Measuring a block of wood, this second grader has reached Piaget's third, or "concrete operational," stage. During this period, which lasts from approximately age seven until 11, the child is able to understand notions of structure and dimensions. However, he is still not capable of more abstract thought.

This learning and modifying of concepts continues throughout life. Adults, as much as children, reform and refine their ideas about the world, changing basic concepts as they go. Consequently, concepts not only mean different things to different people, they also differ from time to time in the same person. "My concept of a 'gene' or a 'seductress' or of President Eisenhower is certainly not the same as it was ten years ago," wrote Arthur Koestler, "though the verbal label attached to each of these concepts has remained the same." Koestler went on to note that words sometimes remain the same while the concepts they embrace can alter from one historical age to another. "It is strange to reflect that a major part of our scientific and philosophical vocabulary consists of old Greek bottles filled and refilled with new wine; that electron once meant a piece of amber and Homer's cosmos a flat disc covered by a vault."

Even though concepts are constantly changing and may mean different things to different people, their importance cannot be exaggerated. Man's ability to make sense out of his experience depends upon his ability to conceptualize—to create what psychologist Roger Brown has called "a theory of reality from the shifting data of perception." Similarly, the historian, concerned with explaining human experience on a broader scale, creates his portrait of the past by formulating a theory of reality from the accumulation of data at his disposal. From his reading and thinking, the historian shapes—and perhaps reshapes and modifies many times—a concept of what made people of a particular historical period act the way they did. He may balance evidence of greed, cupidity and political corruption against other evidence of generosity, selflessness and idealism—all of which are concepts, too—before his overriding concept of men and their motivations solidifies. The historian will doubtless also check and recheck his material against his guiding concept of historical causality—his theory of why one event led to another and that in turn to a third and a fourth. Without some such overall concept to guide him as he wrote, his history would be little more than an account of isolated and unconnected events —a picture of pure accident and hardly a useful or meaningful view of the record of mankind.

The ability to conceptualize also lies at the heart of all scientific endeavor. The reduction of chaos into meaningful order is the goal of scientific effort, and it is here perhaps that the key role of concepts is most evident. One of the greatest scientific achievements in history was Sir Isaac Newton's concept of the interrelation between gravity and the motions of bodies that led to his law of universal gravitation. The old story that the notion came to him when a ripe apple fell from a tree onto his head is almost certainly a romantic invention. But whether he was bombarded by apples or not, Newton observed that all bodies tend to fall to earth. The earth, then, must possess some sort of attraction to objects like apples that forces them to fall. But if this concept is true, why then does the moon not fall toward the earth? The answer to this enigma was necessarily that some force kept the moon sailing along in its orbit. That force, Newton conjectured,

A hurried strategy caucus of Arab diplomats at the United Nations demands concentrated, abstract thinking under pressure. Meeting in June 1967, during the Six-Day Arab-Israeli War, these delegates evaluate old concepts and develop new ones as their give-and-take discussion attempts to reach a consensus on a proposal for a cease-fire.

had to be the motion of the heavenly body—its revolution around the earth must provide enough inertial force to offset exactly its tendency to be attracted by the earth's gravity.

Newton's concept of gravitation is, of course, basic to physics and engineering. Its utility was dramatically demonstrated 300 years after Newton formulated it by artificial satellites and space travel. The reason spacecraft can orbit the earth is that they are lofted at sufficient speed to offset the earth's gravitational pull. To cause a spaceship to descend—as Newton would have understood   it only has to be slowed so that gravity can pull it earthward.

Science has advanced with great speed since Newton's day through the process of concept formation and refinement. Often the concepts arrived at by modern physics have been highly abstract. For example, no one has ever seen an atom, let alone the still smaller electrons, protons and neutrons that it contains. Yet the conclusion that these particles exist is inescapable; the concepts of atoms and their components provide the only possible explanation for many incontrovertible experimental observations of the way in which matter behaves.

Few minds are creative enough to perform the conceptual feats required to discover a new, basic law of nature. It takes a genius like a Newton or an Einstein to comprehend the data pertaining to some large mystery of the universe and then to formulate a theoretical concept sufficiently inclusive to explain all aspects of the mystery. But at all levels of human experience, the mind works through concepts to sort out Roger Brown's "shifting data of perception."

The perception and the sifting process may differ greatly from one part of the world to another. Not all thought is—or ever has been—as ruthlessly logical and purposeful as that of the modern scientist or historian. Such rigorous refining and rejecting of concepts has been characteristic only of certain societies and in certain periods of history. Many minds, and some religions, are content to entertain simultaneously ideas that apparently contradict one another. The idea of a benevolent God, for example, can live alongside a clear realization that the world is a place full of misery and suffering. The thinking of many peoples, especially in the Orient, is not concerned with rationalizing observations. It deals with contemplation of the unknowable, fathomless mysteries of human existence. But it is no less conceptual than Western thought. The concepts that are contemplated are different, but conceptual thinking, here and elsewhere, is a characteristic of the human mind.

The question remains why the mind of the child, the adolescent or the adult creates concepts—indeed, seems driven by some deep impulse to form them. The answer given by Piaget is that the human mind oscillates between states of equilibrium and disequilibrium. When a new fact or observation comes to a person's attention it puts his mind, so to speak, off balance. The new information is not accounted for—it does not fit in with the concepts the mind has already formed. The person's mental model of the world suddenly does not fit the actual world he sees. He becomes troubled and irritated and his mind goes to work to absorb the fresh information —or reject it—and restore a state of mental equilibrium. The mind, to Piaget, is constantly acting, reaching out, experimenting to achieve a state of balance between stimuli coming in from the outer world and the individual's inner world. It is a constant digestive process as natural and inevitable as the physiological digestion of food. This process continues throughout life; the experience of the morning's newspaper will often cause the commuting businessman to undergo some mental disequilibrium as news items challenge his concepts of political behavior and truth and force him to modify some of his opinions.

Such a theory as to why humans form concepts seems to be directly related to drive and stimulus, response and reward—the key elements in conditioned learning *(Chapter 2)*. The upsetting stimulus of new information causes the drive to regain mental equilibrium. The response is the formation of a new concept or the modification of an old one, and the reinforcement is the sense of intellectual achievement. It would appear that these main avenues of learning—conditioning and concept learning —are closely involved with each other.

The researches of Piaget and other students of the learning process, however, have firmly established a very important point—that man is born with a mind that is incurably vital, active and investigative on its own. There was a time when psychology was so dominated by theories of conditioning that the mind as an independent entity was almost ignored, or was assumed to be shaped entirely by outside forces. Human beings were envisioned as passive organisms being acted upon by their surroundings, their behavior the pure product of conditioning forces and with all learning, so to speak, being stamped on the mind from outside. Piaget and others have insisted, on the contrary, that the mind possesses an innate order-generating capacity, a built-in drive to learn. As one psychologist put it, their work has been "a necessary corrective to the oversimplified theory that conditioning explains all learning." It appears instead that conceptualization and conditioning coexist, and that these powerful forces combine to enable the human mind to learn.

The Act of Remembering

4

Among the most amazing people who ever lived was a Russian newspaper reporter, known only as S. in the annals of clinical psychology, who was afflicted with a rare aberration—or perhaps endowed with a rare gift—he seldom forgot anything he saw or heard, no matter how trivial. Most people have selective memories; they remember some things but forget most of what they have encountered. Not S. His mind was encyclopedic: according to the Soviet psychologist A. R. Luria, when S. was given a list of 70 unrelated items he could repeat them perfectly, forward or backward, and not just immediately but weeks, months or years afterward.

In fact S. was so remarkable that he soon gave up newspaper reporting to become a mnemonist, a memory expert who performed on stage. One of his theatrical acts was to listen to the recital of a long list of nonsense syllables—groups of letters with no meaning—by someone in the audience and then to write the entire list on a blackboard from memory. He did this three times a night. His memory was so tenacious that he remembered not only the list read him during each performance but also the lists given him at previous performances.

S.'s memory was not limited to recalling nonsense syllables or other verbal matter, but extended to vision and sound as well. In fact S.'s memory was intensified through a phenomenon known as synesthesia, or crossover of the senses. Certain words produced color and touch sensations every time he heard them. So did musical tones. A tone pitched at 50 cycles and played at a loudness of 100 decibels caused him to see against a dark background a brown strip with "red tonguelike edges." At the same time he experienced a taste of sweet-and-sour borsch over his entire tongue. Changing the pitch transformed the image into a "velvet cord with fibers jutting out on all sides" and a still higher pitch and louder volume caused his mind to conjure up a whisk broom of fiery color giving off sparks. On meeting someone, Professor Luria's subject would often be so preoccupied with the color of the person's voice—which could be yellow, red or purple—that he could not follow what was being said. S. gave synesthesia credit for much of the power of his phenomenal memory; his mind, he explained, naturally turned a list of simple and unrelated items into stirring, related images that were far easier for him to remember.

The story of S., the man who forgot nothing, underlines the enormous potential of human memory. Most people cannot achieve anything that comes even close to S.'s powers, but the ordinary memory is nonetheless one of the most remarkable aspects of the human mind. During a lifetime the average person's memory can store billions of items, including more than 50,000 words and an even larger file of pictures—faces, scenes, objects. Although only a few of these items are consciously present in the mind at any given moment, a remarkable range of facts, images, concepts and verbal expressions can be retrieved from the memory's vast storehouse of material. This may be done with considerable effort or with unexpected ease. Or it may be triggered accidentally by a stray encounter, which will bring stored information from the depths of the mind to the threshold of awareness. How the three-pound, striated blob of jelly that comprises the human brain can retain and use this library of information with its myriad sensory associations is one of the marvels and mysteries of human life.

The major importance of human memory is its role in learning. Indeed memory and learning are inseparable; learning cannot occur without the retention and recall of past experience. The role of memory in learning has been well expressed by science writer Will Bradbury in a LIFE article on the brain. If man had no memory, Bradbury says, he "could do little more than fumble with the sensory inputs of the moment. Without memory, man's extraordinary powers for putting things into groups, for relating likes and unlikes, for generating options and hypotheses, for creating the complicated fabric of his life, simply would not exist."

In view of the importance of memory to learning, and thus to all human life, it is not surprising that psychologists have devoted much time and energy to its study. They have investigated the way in which the memory acquires material, and the reasons why some things are remembered while others are forgotten. They have also probed the means through which long-remembered facts or impressions can be brought to the forefront of the conscious mind. Closely related has been the effort to determine why certain items stubbornly elude recall and what forces interfere with the memory's operations. Although a full understanding of all the aspects of something as complex as memory may always escape them, psychologists have made impressive strides toward understanding how humans remember, why they forget and why they remember some things better than others.

Modern psychology divides memory into three systems, each with its own powers and peculiarities. One is sensory memory—the remembered smell of a perfume's odor, the touch of a certain fabric, the sight of a face or a landscape. The second is motor-skill memory—the remembered feel of doing something physical such as riding a bicycle. The third is what psychologists call verbal memory, which includes everything a person has heard, read or thought: words, ideas, concepts.

The first two systems—those for sensory impressions and motor skills —are phenomenally retentive. Sensory memory is especially powerful. Most people, psychologists say, retain images of virtually everything that has ever captured their attention. The cliché apology, "I remember your face but I can't recall the name," expresses a truth; most people literally never forget the face of a person they have met, even if they saw him only once and decades before. The power of visual memory has been demonstrated in the laboratory by Ralph Haber of the University of Rochester's psychology department. He flashed thousands of slides for 10 seconds each before a group of volunteers. Then he showed the group several hundred pairs of pictures, each pair containing one of the slides already shown. Haber's subjects correctly picked the image they had seen so briefly better than 85 per cent of the time.

People's recognition of scenes is sometimes so vivid that it approaches hallucination. Almost everybody has rounded a curve in a road and seen before him a landscape that he is positive he has seen before—although he is equally positive he has never been on that particular road. The explanation appears to be that this new landscape contains features reminiscent of another landscape that the person has in fact seen previously. The visual memory for such scenes can be so powerful that the similarity causes a spark to jump, so to speak, in the brain, connecting old with new and giving the viewer a haunting sense of recognition and familiarity. The common term for this sort of impression is *déjà vu*, French for "already seen," and recorded examples of such impressions go far back in time. Two and a half millennia ago Plato, recognizing that most people have moments of *déjà vu*, argued that such occurrences are real memories of events that took place in a previous existence and prove that people have lived another life before this one.

Another supercharged form of visual memory is what psychologists call eidetic imagery and everybody else terms photographic memory. Some people are able, in effect, to mentally photograph a picture or a page of text and remember every detail. If a normal person looks at a painting and then looks away at a blank wall, he will be able to describe the picture in general terms. But the individual with eidetic memory can actually project the entire image onto the wall and describe any detail in the picture perfectly. History provides many examples of people with remarkably powerful photographic memories. Leonardo da Vinci could draw a detailed portrait of a person after meeting him once, and Napoleon could glance at a military map and know every stream, town or hillock on it.

Such remarkably acute visual memories have parallels in the auditory realm, especially among great musicians. Beethoven, Mozart and Wagner were able to re-create in their heads the texture and sound of an entire orchestra playing a symphony. In modern times the great conductor Arturo Toscanini could remember a score after one or two hearings and write it out from memory 40 years later. The pianist Walter Gieseking, who disliked practicing, was known for his phenomenal memory. On one occasion he promised a composer that he would play one of his compositions as an encore. Gieseking forgot all about it until the day of the concert. In his dressing room during the intermission he glanced over the seven- or eight-

page score. Then he went on stage, performed the second part of his recital and wound up playing the entire promised score from memory.

Few people possess such extraordinary memories as these, but everybody remembers myriad items of sensory experience. These stored impressions are vital to learning—they are part, at least, of the material from which people construct concepts and therefore think. The raw material of the world is collected by the senses and it is from this raw material in large part that the intellect abstracts its generalizations and rules as it imposes order on the flux of experience.

The second form of memory identified by psychologists is the retention and the seemingly automatic recall after long intervals of motor skills learned early in life. As the human being grows from infancy he must learn and remember a wide range of muscular and nervous responses —how to walk, how to grasp objects, how to arrange and rearrange the muscles of the mouth and throat so that speech is possible. Motor-skill memory is extremely tenacious; once learned, such skills are virtually never forgotten. A person who learned as a child to ride a bicycle retains into old age the ability to balance himself on a bike. A person who has once learned to ice skate or to swim can always skate or swim. Certain motor skills can become rusty—a pilot who has not flown for 10 years will need a refresher course. But the skill is soon relearned. The motor responses are still there, needing only a few practice sessions to become sharp once more.

The third main category, what psychologists call semantic or verbal memory, makes it possible for man to embrace organized bodies of knowledge. Some people have prodigious powers of recall for this kind of material. The late Irwin Edman, long a professor of philosophy at Columbia University, was able to quote dozens of lines of poetry that he had scanned only once and to remember with uncanny accuracy the contents of virtually every book that he had ever read. Edman, who had weak eyesight, offered a tongue-in-cheek explanation for his powers of recall: with his bad eyes he could not afford to read anything twice.

Verbal memory, most scientists today agree, can be divided into two systems. The first is known as active memory and consists of the variegated impulses that crowd the mind in its everyday contact with the environment. This memory is useful but transient. When the average person looks in the directory for a telephone number, for example, he remembers the number for the seconds it takes to dial the phone; then the number drops out of the brain's mental "hold" and is lost forever. Active memory of this kind is often called short-term memory.

The other kind of verbal memory is, of course, known as long-term memory. This is the sort of memory that retains material for months, years, a lifetime. It is the type of memory that makes learning possible. If a student could not recall that two and two are four, or that Shakespeare wrote plays, or that Napoleon was the self-proclaimed Emperor of France, then he obviously could make little progress in the study of mathematics, English literature or European history.

The key to remembering things that need to be retained over long periods is the ability somehow to shunt material off the busy merry-go-round of short-term memory and into the long-term vault. The student who needs to remember what he has read or heard in school and the businessman who must recall the vital facts of a business deal are both faced with the problem of converting the evanescent impression into a permanent acquisition.

This vital area of memory mechanics, not surprisingly, has attracted the attention of many psychologists. They have studied factors that may frustrate the conversion of short-term into long-term memory and the circumstances or techniques that may facilitate the process.

One impediment to successful memorization is a species of mental interference or static. The businessman preparing for an important conference tries to memorize the facts and figures pertaining to a complex negotiation. Having mastered these details, he then turns to the facts involved in a second transaction. Unless he possesses a remarkably retentive memory, he will find that memorizing the facts of deal No. 2 will make him for-

get some elements of deal No. 1. He will have to return to the first set of papers and review them again.

Psychologists call this sort of interference "retroactive inhibition," and they have demonstrated in their laboratories that it happens to everybody. In an oft-repeated experiment, a group of volunteer subjects is asked to memorize list A, a string of words or nonsense syllables. One half of the subjects are then told to memorize list B while the other half rests. After a period of time both groups are asked to write down list A. Invariably the group that simply rested remembers list A far better than the people who memorized list B; the second memorizing task has interfered with the first one. A similar effect occurs when the tasks are reversed. If half of the subjects learn list A while the other half rests, and then both groups learn list B, the subjects who rested, not having learned list A, will remember B more accurately; prior learning may also interfere with new learning.

These experiments may suggest that multiple memorization tasks are doomed to failure because the material is bound to collide and become a confused jumble. Actually, such experiments have helped point the way toward better memorization. A key factor is time. Psychologists giving the list-A-list-B type of test have discovered that the performance improves if the volunteer subjects are allowed extra time between the two learning processes. The lesson is clear: the person memorizing material should take time for a little mental rest after doing task No. 1 and before tackling task No. 2. This gives the mind time to consolidate the material, moving at least some of it from short-term into long-term memory.

The effectiveness of this strategy was supported by an experiment performed on, of all things, cockroaches. Roaches were placed on a partially electrified laboratory tray and conditioned by electric shocks to avoid one corner of the tray. Then half of the roaches were placed in a dark damp spot, which apparently is a roach's idea of heaven. There the insects became comatose. Meanwhile, the other half were placed in a hot, brightly lighted spot, which made them hyperactive. After a period of time both groups were returned to the original tray. The group that had been quiet excelled in remembering to shun the electrified part of the tray; the hyperactive group, however, had forgotten their previous learning and ran about aimlessly, receiving shocks. Aside from demonstrating the ingenuity of psychologists in conceiving experiments, the cockroach caper supports the idea that rest after a learning task promotes retention.

If rest does promote retention, then how about sleep? Some psychologists have found, in fact, that human memory retention is greater when learning is followed by a nap or a night's sleep than when it is followed by the hurly-burly of everyday activities. Dreams may also help. Psychologists have theorized that they are in part a mechanism through which the mind sorts out the impressions of the previous day. The kaleidoscope of the dream may, by bringing up trivial and meaningless material, effectively get rid of it, thus helping the memory to absorb only learning that is useful. So little is yet established about the connections between memories and dreams, however, that at present this remains an intriguing theory.

Other studies of the mechanisms by which the mind absorbs and retains information have shown that the greater the similarity between two learning tasks, the greater the memory interference. If lists A and B are much alike, the test subjects have difficulty retaining them accurately. A student who is taking two language courses, in other words, should not study his French vocabulary lists and then shift immediately to learning Latin nouns. The two lists will interfere with each other. Instead, the student should break up his study pattern—work on the French assignment for an hour, perhaps, and then, after a few minutes of time off, open his history book, or study mathematics awhile before turning to his Latin.

Memorization tests like these have also furnished evidence that material is acquired faster and retained more accurately if it is meaningful. Subjects who were given lists of real words to memorize have done better than subjects provided with lists of nonsense syllables, and subjects given sensible grammatical sentences to commit to memory have performed even better. This seems so obvious as to be a truism. But it has important implications, for memorizing and for teaching. The instructor will be far more successful in getting his students to learn if he provides them with some sort of framework into which they can fit the facts that they need to memorize. A teacher of 19th Century European history, for example, might have little success if he demanded that his students learn by rote a list reading, "Battle of Waterloo and Congress of Vienna, 1815; Revolutions of 1830 and 1848; Commune of 1871." He would doubtless have greater success if he showed that these names and dates can make a pattern, explaining that in the same year as Napoleon's 1815 defeat at Waterloo many diplomats met in Vienna to restore European order after years of Napoleonic wars. Then he might add that the Congress of Vienna, by attempting to clamp a lid on the social changes that followed the wars, provoked a trio of generally unsuccessful revolutions, one in 1830, one in 1848 and the third in 1871. This sort of approach provides what psychologists call meaningful context, and is of great pedagogical value.

The individual attempting to learn something on his own can apply a comparable technique called, plainly enough, principle learning. One psychological investigator describes this method as simply "finding a logical pattern in the material we want to retain." He goes on to explain that identification numbers of various sorts—Social Security numbers, Army serial numbers, and the like—"have to be learned by rote since they have no intrinsic meaning; but meaningful patterns of one kind or another can be found in most material that is worth remembering. The way to remember a play or a novel is to concentrate on the plot and fit the details into this framework. . . . It is almost always easier to remember a principle than to remember the details; and we can usually work out the details from the principle that brings them together."

The last important techniques that psychologists recommend for converting information—even rote material—from short-term to long-term memory are self-recitation and periodic review. Self-recitation means only that the person should test himself as he goes along through the material to be learned, or as soon as he has finished reading it. If he cannot answer the questions he asks himself, he should go back to the relevant parts of the book immediately. Psychologists maintain that asking oneself questions about the material just covered is more effective than a second complete reading or even a third. Self-recitation is a more active occupation than reading and stimulates the processes of memory and recall.

Periodic review obviously is an aid to memorization. But experiments have demonstrated that certain kinds of review are far more helpful than others. First of all, psychologists say, the review sessions should begin shortly after the chapter is finished or the theorem studied since people tend to forget most rapidly soon after the initial exposure to the material. Second, frequent review periods, even though short, will fix the matter to be learned far more effectively in long-term memory than infrequent but lengthy cramming sessions. In fact, it is a truism of psychological learning theory that short periods of carefully spaced practice are a better way to learn anything, from tennis to trigonometry, than cram sessions. It is perhaps futile for parents to hope that their school-age children can be persuaded to give up last-minute cramming and institute a regular schedule of review sessions; it would seem to go against human nature, or juvenile nature at least. But it might be worth almost any amount of persuasion to avoid the traumas of pre-exam panic, and it might make the entire educational process more enjoyable for the student.

The utility of frequent review as an aid to memorization is underlined by the power of what psychologists call "relearning"—it is far easier to learn and remember material that has been partially learned before. Familiarity breeds retention. If a student quickly scans a history text, getting the broad outlines of the period under study, and then, perhaps a week later, buckles down to closer study, he will find that the details lodge in mind and memory more quickly and firmly.

Psychologist Harold Burtt of Ohio State University demonstrated this point with an intriguing experiment. He read aloud three passages from Greek literature to his two-year-old son. The child understood not a word of the readings. Then, when the child was eight, Burtt gave the child the same three passages and three new ones to memorize. The child performed better on the passages that had been read to him at an earlier age than on passages he had never heard. Even such early exposure to material that was not understood had left at least a faint trace in the memory.

Devices and schemes to improve the memory are enormously popular. Most of them involve some forms of organization and association. One of the devices recommended in a recent (and best-selling) American book by the memory specialist Harry Lorayne and basketball ace Jerry Lucas, a memory-scheme enthusiast, is to attach what one wants to remember to a ridiculous scene, the more unusual the better. In memorizing, say, a list of animals, it helps to place the animals in absurd mental pictures. If the rhinoceros and the gorilla are among the animals on the list, imagine a rhino playing on a harp, and then place the gorilla in your bed. The comic images help the memory retain the list of animals.

Such devices, called mnemonics, are a technique that goes back to the Greeks. According to the great Roman orator Cicero, the poet Simonides of Ceos was sitting at a banquet table with a number of guests when he had to leave the room. While he was out the roof of the hall collapsed, crushing everyone at the banquet to death. The bodies around the table were so mangled that relatives and friends were unable to claim them. Simonides, it is told, thereupon was able to identify all the bodies through his memory of the places where they had sat around the table. Simonides realized that the use of organization and pattern in the mind pointed to a technique of remembering that would prove valuable to the political orators of the time, who gave their speeches from memory. He thereupon invented the art of mnemonics and evidently became the consultant of the leading orators of his day.

Simonides' use of places, or loci, in association with words and images is still one of the leading techniques in memory-improvement. If a person wishes to remember the names of the members of a Congressional committee, he should find a way after the fashion of Simonides to tie them to their seat locations in a hearing room. A speech can be remembered more easily by associating parts of the speech with the known locations of furniture and other familiar objects in a room. The Greeks, it is said, designed special buildings full of memorable loci where orators could practice their speeches. In medieval times charts were devised that contained pictures of many loci. By associating various topics with the pictures, a priest was aided in remembering all the parts of a long sermon.

More recently a variation of the mnemonic device has been recommended by Lorayne and Lucas as an aid in committing people's names to memory. The device is to invent substitute rhyming or punning words for the person's real name, and then to associate it with a mental image. If the man introduced at the cocktail party is named Cameron, the trick is to mentally change the name to "camera on" and form a mental image of a motion-picture camera whirling. If the name is Krakowitz, make it "cracker wits" and imagine a box of biscuits. Oppenheim becomes "open home," a bilingual play on words since *Heim* is "home" in German.

Similar tricks, Lorayne and Lucas say, can be used to help memorize the words of a foreign language. Beans in French are *haricots;* the learner imagines beans wearing hairy coats. Snails are *escargots,* which can be imagined as a gigantic snail carrying a cargo of S's—S-cargo. Or the same device can be used to memorize facts about the arts. To recall that Wagner composed *Tannhäuser,* for example, the student might imagine a wagon crashing into a townhouse. The basis of all of their mnemonic devices, Lorayne and Lucas say, is to associate any new piece of information to be learned "with something you already know or remember."

A prodigious memory for names and faces enabled U.S. protocol chief Angier Biddle Duke (second from right) to present hundreds of individuals in White House reception lines to government officials without faltering. Here Duke presents guests to Secretary of State Dean Rusk and India's Jawaharlal Nehru.

The only trouble with such clever mnemonic tricks is that they may sometimes be so elaborate that they are harder to learn than the material to be memorized. Struggling to discover associative links, the memorizer may clutter up his head with a system of far-fetched, burdensome and irrelevant details. Further, psychologists have demonstrated that the overall power of the memory cannot be improved simply through more and more memorization. The memory is not a muscle that can be developed by exercise. Is it worth all the trouble and effort the mnemonists recommend to be able to commit to memory a great many facts that might just as well go in an address book or a desk file?

It may be possible to improve the ways the memory acquires or learns material, but this does not solve several other problems concerning the operation of memory. One is the question of memory loss: how does it happen that certain material that has been committed to long-term memory and has remained accessible for long periods—many months or even many years—often becomes inaccessible later? Another question is why people remember certain important things they have learned but are unable to recall other, apparently equally vital pieces of information.

There are a number of theories as to why long-term memories can no longer be recalled. One initially plausible theory holds that the memory fades or decays through disuse until it eventually vanishes entirely. Evidence suggests, however, that this explanation may be unsatisfactory, or at least incomplete. For example, elderly people often find that they are able to recall incidents from their childhood that had disappeared from their memories for decades. The memory has persisted; the changes that take place in the brain with advancing age make it available again. Another objection to the theory that memory decays through disuse is the fact that people who have emigrated from their native land and have become fluent in the language of their adopted country often revert when ill and delirious to their original tongue, which they may not have spoken for 50 years or more.

Another piece of evidence that seems to prove that memories do not simply atrophy stems from hypnosis and psychoanalysis. Under hypnosis a person can be made to blurt out memories that his mind cannot recover when he is awake. The memories are still there and hypnosis merely opens the gates. In a 1959 experiment, psychologists found that adults under hypnosis could remember far more about their early schooling—the name of their second-grade teacher and the students who sat at nearby desks, for example—than they could recall in a waking state.

The skilled psychoanalyst can, over a period of months, perform the same function as the hypnotist. Gently prodding his patient, the analyst helps him, so to speak, to undertake an archeological dig down into his memory, uncovering layer after layer of buried experiences until the patient reaches that deeply suppressed level of painful material that has been causing him psychic pain, irrational fears or neurotic symptoms.

A further reason to conclude that memory traces do not simply decay is that all people, at one time or another, have had the experience often called the "Proustian moment." This is the sudden flash of recall of some memory apparently long since forgotten that takes a person completely by surprise. It is named after French novelist Marcel Proust, the greatest creative writer to analyze memory and the mysteries of recall. Proust's masterpiece, the seven-volume series of novels called *Remembrance of Things Past,* is a long hymn to the miracle of memory as well as an analysis of its mechanism. The experiences that triggered recall for Proust were sensory ones—smells, sounds, the feel of a certain piece of pavement under foot or the sight of a room. Such stimuli conjured up full-blown past experiences with all their details, almost physically transporting him back over the gulf of years. Having been whisked backward in time, Proust found that other memories would start to come into focus. He concluded that each person can "develop" the "negatives" of such memories, to bring to full consciousness the dim images long ago registered by the mind. To recapture all of one's past through memory, Proust said, is the only way to make meaning of one's life, to see what all that past experience meant.

Not everyone has the perseverance to systematically recover all his past memories, let alone record the process in a 1,400,000-word novel. But everyone experiences that magical, involuntary but complete recall—the Proustian moment—sometimes triggered by a particular smell or sight or sound. The distinguished psychologist Neal Miller has reported an interesting variant of this sort of unbidden recall. A native of the state of Washington, he returned home each summer for his vacation. When his schedule was altered by World War II duties, he made his annual visit in the fall. He found that autumn sights and smells flooded him with vivid memories of childhood, memories not conjured up by previous summer visits. Miller concluded that he had become used to summer sights and smells so that they no longer set off trains of memory—in fact, the newer experiences of summer interfered with old memories—but the novelty of the fall visit made his memory leap over all the intervening years.

If sensory triggers almost by chance can arouse old memories that are remarkably detailed and loaded with vivid emotions, then it would seem that people's minds must contain vast stores of such memories. This appears to be the case. Dr. Wilder Penfield, a leading brain surgeon, has used an electric probe during brain operations to locate the area of brain damage. As he has touched areas of the brain with his probe, the patients, under a local anesthetic and therefore awake during this part of the operation, have experienced the most vivid and detailed re-creations of scenes

Feats of memory retrieval are a source of pride for this group of first-graders in Carson, California, who eagerly raise their hands in response to their teacher's questions about telling time. Having explained the minute and hour hands, she calls for a volunteer, then flashes the make-believe clock and asks for the time.

from their past lives. In other words, the mild electric shock has energized and released these otherwise lost memories. It is reasonable to suppose from this evidence that memories are much more permanently etched on man's brain than one might assume. It is even possible that virtually everything that has ever happened to a person is inscribed somewhere in memory. But the vast bulk of this matter cannot be recalled unless there is a powerful stimulus, and therefore much of it remains buried.

Most psychologists believe that the problem is not one of fading or decaying memories, but that impediments block the recapturing of material stored in the mind. Recall may often be frustrated, they say, because of what they have dubbed "cue" trouble. The right cue, or stimulus, has simply not been available at the time of attempted recall. "Long-term memory storage," say psychologists Ernest Hilgard, Richard Atkinson and Rita Atkinson in their *Introduction to Psychology*, "is analogous to a filing cabinet of large capacity. As any file clerk knows, it is one thing to toss items into various file drawers; it is a more difficult task to retrieve a desired item." They go on to give an example: a city council might get a letter from a Mr. Johnson complaining about water pollution. Is the letter filed under "Johnson," "complaints," "sanitation" or "pollution"? In like fashion, the memory may, in effect, code material under only one or two headings. If the right cue word does not come to the person's attention, the memory, although it still exists somewhere in the mind, is not elicited.

Cue trouble may help explain a common phenomenon—why students sometimes do badly on examinations even though they have studied quite hard. It may be that the students have committed the course material to memory under headings that seem meaningful to them. But then the examination questions take another tack, asking the students to comment on the material from an entirely different angle. The cues that were expected do not appear and although the student searches his mind an extensive part of the material cannot be retrieved.

Another theory holds that people frequently forget what they want to forget, mainly unpleasant experiences. Such blocking of the recall process usually operates on an unconscious level. The mind, rather than be perpetually burdened with unpleasant memories, contrives to suppress them.

Unpleasant tasks, for instance, tend to fade out of memory. To take a simple example, shoveling snow is a laborious, often exhausting chore. Householders in snowy northern climes are cordially sick of it by March, if not by New Year's. And yet the next November, when the first snow flies, people become excited by its beauty of the promise of pleasant experiences like skiing. They may recall that snow also presages a return to the hated shovel, but the grimness of the task has dimmed in memory.

This principle has significance for learning and education. If school is an unpleasant experience for a child, then what he is taught there is not likely to be retained in his memory. Too often schools convert learning, which should be exciting, into pointless drudgery, extinguishing joy—and with it the hope of remembering the material that is supposed to be learned.

The rejection of distasteful or painful experiences can take the extreme form of amnesia, a total rejection of facts. A classic case that made headlines in the United States some years ago was that of an Akron, Ohio, salesman who disappeared under suspicious circumstances, leaving a pregnant wife, three children and a worrisome load of debts. A fishing boat he had rented was found empty on the shore of a lake and the police assumed he had drowned. Eight years later he was discovered in a city in the West, with a new name, career, wife and two children. He said he had no memory of his life in Akron. The story was hard to believe. As a shrewd observer asked, how could the memory of family and debts go blank while the subject retained all the faculties required by a new career? However, intensive investigation proved the legitimacy of this rare case of amnesia and the victim was eventually allowed to remain in his new life. Evidently he had blanked out on his life in Akron because there were aspects of it that were simply too painful for him to remember.

The human mind often distorts or represses memories because they are so deeply associated with guilt and anxiety that the conscious mind cannot tolerate them. As Freud found during analyses of his neurotic patients, material that is too distressing or painful is thrust downward and buried in the subconscious. The backbone of Freud's therapeutic technique, of course, was to encourage a patient to delve for these painful memories and neutralize their baneful influence by articulating them. One way that Freud went about getting at this otherwise inaccessible material was to persuade the patient to free-associate, articulating whatever random thoughts and memories might come to mind. Freud's hope was to pluck out clues from this rambling discourse that would lead to the buried memories that were causing the trouble. His other technique was to encourage the patient to remember and retell his dreams. In the fantasy world of dreams Freud also picked up clues pointing to suppressed material.

Many people have suffered the neurotic amnesia that Freud—and his many successors—have tried to penetrate. Everyone experiences another kind of amnesia, however, an inability to remember the first two or three years of life. Some memory remains of these years; after all, this is when people begin to walk and talk. But scenes and events that occurred during these years vanish from the mind. Freud found that through analysis he could sometimes enable a patient to remember further back into his youth than he had been able to do before. So some forgetting of early childhood memories may be the result of repression. But the bulk of childhood amnesia probably comes from a very young child's inability to organize his memories for specific events and thus cling to them.

When a child has passed the boundaries of childhood amnesia at about age three he begins to retain more and more memories. Why memory develops at this point in the child's life has been analyzed by the Swiss psychologist Jean Piaget. Piaget's theory is that memory begins when the child develops the ability to organize what he sees and feels into some kind of order. The very young child sees the world as one unrelated phe-

A frail and sensitive young writer, Marcel Proust at 30 was a frequent guest at fashionable French salons. A few years later he became a recluse and devoted the remaining years of his life to the composition of his monumental novel Remembrance of Things Past.

A memorable taste of things past

In a key passage from *Remembrance of Things Past,* Proust recalls how the sensory experience of a snack of tea and sponge cake released a flood of childhood memories of vacations at Combray. A condensed version of the text is reproduced below.

Many years had elapsed during which nothing of Combray had any existence for me, when one day in winter, as I came home, my mother, seeing that I was cold, offered me some tea, a thing I did not ordinarily take. She sent out for those short, plump little cakes called petites madeleines and soon I raised to my lips a spoonful of the tea in which I had soaked a morsel of the cake. No sooner had the warm liquid, and the crumbs with it, touched my palate than a shudder ran through my whole body, and I stopped, intent upon the extraordinary changes that were taking place. An exquisite pleasure had invaded my senses, but individual, detached, with no suggestion of its origin. In that moment all the flowers in our garden and in Mr. Swann's park and the good folk of the village and their little dwellings and the parish church and the whole of Combray sprang into being, town and gardens alike, from my cup of tea.

nomenon after another. But at some point the capacity to organize his world emerges. Only then, when impressions and experiences begin to make sense, to cohere in meaningful patterns, does the child begin to construct memories that last and can be recalled in later years. If arranging experience into meaningful wholes helps the adult to remember, the same power is essential for childhood memory.

The beginnings of memory in childhood may also have something to do with language. Before language ability develops the child has no way to catalogue and store memories. With language, however, the child finds that he has labels to identify the concepts that he is beginning to form. In short, the world becomes more organized and meaningful—and as a consequence easier to remember.

The study of certain adult amnesia victims furnished psychologists with some understanding of the process of forgetting. George Talland of Massachusetts General Hospital in Boston has reported on his study of 17 patients suffering from Korsakoff's syndrome, loss of memory resulting from the brain damage caused by acute alcoholism. He read a passage from a newspaper to these patients and then to a group of normal people with no memory disorder. The opening sentences of the passage read:

"In a city in India several thousand school children paraded in the main square to celebrate the sixty-eighth birthday of the prime minister. While reviewing the parade the prime minister released a number of doves, the symbols of peace, from the cages in which they had been kept."

Talland found that the Korsakoff syndrome patients distorted the news item with far greater regularity and with more substantive error than the normal people. For instance, a large percentage of the amnesiacs reported that the "prime minister had 68 doves to celebrate his birthday." Talland regards this distortion as an example of how the memory frequently fails to retain all of what has been seen or heard and instead tries to reconstruct the information from remembered bits and pieces. Unfortunately those with brain damage do not retain enough of the bits and pieces to reconstruct an accurate account of what they have heard.

It is interesting to note, however, that when Talland asked normal people to pass the same item of information from one to another over the phone, they tended in the process to distort the content in much the same way as the Korsakoff disease patients. Some people made up their own numbers (say 5,000 children or 68 doves) while others made up their own contexts (the children released the doves). Evidently there is a similar tendency to distort through reconstruction, whether the cues are incomplete or brain damage interferes with reception of the information.

Not all such reconstruction is automatically bad. Professor Frederic C. Bartlett of England's Cambridge University, who devoted many years to the study of how a rumor develops, tells of an experiment in which he told a bizarre folk tale to one student, who was asked to pass it on to another student and so on. The successive versions of the story were indeed distorted, but in the direction of simplicity, better organization, more coherence and removal of irrelevancies. More study is needed to show when reconstruction to fill the gaps of memory becomes dangerous and when it may prove useful. Reorganization of material is a vital part of recall, but in the process the mind may introduce considerable distortion.

For all the time and energy that have been expended on it by psychologists and psychiatrists, memory is still a puzzling subject in many ways. One intriguing mystery is why some people who are experts in a specialty —such as stamp collecting or the collecting and restoring of antiques—can remember every little fact concerning their specialty and yet may have poor memories for everyday matters. The great inventor Thomas Edison is said to have once forgotten his own name when an official suddenly demanded it. The stock figure of the specialist who knows everything there is to know about some abstruse subject and yet mislays his rubbers is the absent-minded professor, the subject of hundreds of humorous stories.

Some of the tales of learned men who suffer from a chronic inability to remember the details of everyday living are probably true enough. One classic case of professorial absent-mindedness (and one vouched for as true) came to light at Harvard some years ago. A most learned man who had written a book at age 28 that had revolutionized his field of study was unable one fall to begin his lectures—his notes were lost. He and his friends searched everywhere in vain for weeks. Finally the precious scribblings were found safely lodged in the professor's refrigerator.

Columbia's Irwin Edman, the savant who had a prodigious memory for what he read, was also an exemplar of absent-mindedness in everyday matters. Edman enjoyed telling the story on himself that one day he encountered some of his students on the route between the university and his home. After a profound discussion of recondite points of philosophy, Edman asked the students whether he had been walking north or south when he met them. "South," said the students. "That's good," said Edman, "that means I've had lunch."

A much-repeated story, told of many absent-minded professors, involves a celebrated pedagogue who was chatting with another professor and his wife after dinner. The talk went on and on until the other professor said, "Well, it's late and I have an early class, so I guess I'll have to ask you to leave." "Heavens," said the absent-minded one, "I thought we were at *my* house and I was about to ask *you* to leave."

The lesson that might be drawn from such stories is that even the highest brows conceal tricky memories. Absent-minded professors and all other people have hierarchies of memory and are consequently able to recall the sorts of material that they think important more readily than others. Perhaps the absent-minded professors have opted for memory of the sort of learning that counts—encyclopedic knowledge of their field of study. This may absorb their attention so exclusively that they are incapable of recalling the practical things that the rest of mankind feels it must remember to get through the normal tasks of living.

Culture as a Teacher

In *The Forest People*, anthropologist Colin Turnbull tells how he came out of the African rain forest with a Pygmy named Kenge and saw some buffalo grazing at a distance. Kenge, who had never been out of the forest before, turned to Turnbull and asked, "What insects are those?"

Psychologists Michael Cole and Sylvia Scribner in *Culture and Thought* relate the story of a 10-year-old Kpelle boy from the hinterland of Liberia who was taken to the capital at Monrovia. The child went to the top of a tall building and saw some tankers out at sea. He had never seen anything like that before, and he remarked that the men who would go to sea in such small boats must surely be brave.

To people accustomed to understanding the perspective of remote vistas, and to Westerners who know what buffalo and ships look like, the identification and perception of the true sizes of distant animals and tankers would present no problem. But the limited experience of the Pygmies and the Kpelle had never provided them with an opportunity to see buffalo and tankers at a distance. They therefore responded to these objects in what would seem to a Westerner to be an unusual way.

Culture and environment can have the same kind of effect with concepts. Another example involving the Kpelle illustrates the point. Two groups of volunteers were assembled in Liberia to take some psychological tests. One group was made up of 60 U.S. Peace Corps members training to serve as teachers, the other of 20 nonliterate adult Kpelle tribesmen. In the first test, everyone was asked to estimate the number of measuring cups of rice in a bowl. The results were striking. The estimates made by the Peace Corps trainees ranged from six to 20 cups; every Kpelle estimated the number to be slightly under nine. The bowl contained exactly nine cups of rice.

In a second test the members of the original Peace Corps group and 30 more Kpelle adults were confronted with eight cards, each of which was marked with numbers and red or green squares or triangles. The instructions were to sort out the cards in matching piles three different ways. Again the results were striking. The Peace Corps volunteers raced through the test without error while the Kpelle had great difficulty sorting the cards.

The tests seem simple enough, but the results are easily misconstrued. "To the casual American observer," commented John Gay and Michael

Cole, the two American investigators who conducted the tests, "the inability of the Kpelle subjects to sort the cards perhaps seems incredible. In fact, it is just this kind of observation that has led men to say 'Africans think like children' or to speak of 'primitive mentality.' But what about the Peace Corps volunteers' performance when asked to make a simple numerical estimate? Would this not appear an inept performance to any normal Kpelle adult?"

Social scientists believe that neither of these conclusions is correct. The key to the discrepancies between the performances of the Kpelle farmers and the Peace Corps volunteers involves not the level of mental ability, but the cultures in which the two peoples were raised. The basic mechanisms involved in learning appear to be the same the world over, no matter whether the subjects are the Kpelle or Peace Corps volunteers, Hottentots or Hopi, Chinese or Czechoslovaks. All human beings learn through conditioning triggered by the stimulus-response-reward mechanism. All learn as well by forming concepts. And all make use of memory for the storage and retrieval of necessary information.

But *what* people learn, *what* they remember and *why* and *how* they go about solving problems do indeed depend upon the environment and the culture in which they are raised and live. The Kpelle excelled in the rice estimates because they are farmers who make their living by growing rice. They measure out rice by the cup, bucket, tin and bag, and they know that there are 100 cups of rice in a bag. If they were not able to estimate amounts of rice accurately, they would be in trouble at the marketplace. On the other hand, nothing in their experience had prepared them to look at a stack of cards and sort them into matching piles.

By contrast, the Peace Corps volunteers—like most people who grow up in Western cultures—were familiar with playing cards. As children they probably had been surrounded with toys and building blocks of various shapes, sizes and colors, which they had learned to organize into categories. In addition, they were aided by their familiarity with the concept of psychological testing, having been subjected to intelligence and other tests throughout their lives. For all these reasons, they could look at a stack of cards and quickly understand how to sort them into piles.

The Kpelle farmers and the Peace Corps volunteers, of course, are products of strikingly different cultures, but both are examples of the process known as enculturation, by which society imparts its skills and values to its members. Every society has its own traditions and special skills, and every society perpetuates itself by passing its values and rules along to its young. Through this process society teaches its standards of conduct; it provides heroes and villains to emulate or scorn, rewards behavior that it approves, and discourages behavior it does not like.

Cultural indoctrination begins at an early age. A baby comes into the world knowing no language, possessing no values and having no conception of the world he lives in. All these skills and concepts are absorbed from people around him.

The lessons by which he learns society's values may be quite simple and direct. On Guadalcanal, in the Solomon Islands, for example, generosity and respect for property are two of the highest social values. A child begins to acquire them almost as soon as he is old enough to pick things up. If he grabs a banana, his parents insist that he share it with a playmate; if he refuses, the parents break it in half and give half to his friend.

If the child meddles with someone else's possessions, he is rebuked immediately: "Put that down. It belongs to so-and-so." If he refuses to obey, the object is snatched from him and returned to its owner. At this stage of the child's life, the lessons in generosity and property rights are taught by simple commands without any explanation. Later, when the child is four or five, the commands are accompanied by verbal explanations. He is told that it is important for children to be considerate of others so that later on they will be respected by their fellow citizens. The lesson includes both of the great learning processes: conditioning through reward and punishment, and concept learning.

Parents, peers, teachers and other authority figures play key roles in imparting values to young children. Even a simple thought conveyed by them at the right moment may make an indelible impression. Bertrand Russell, the English mathematician and philosopher, who died in 1970, tells in his autobiography how a single concept taught him by his grandmother changed his entire life.

Russell's parents had died when he was in infancy, and he was left to his grandmother's care. "My grandmother . . . was the most important person to me throughout my childhood," Russell writes. "She was a Scotch Presbyterian, Liberal in politics and religion (she became a Unitarian at the age of seventy), but extremely strict in all matters of morality."

Russell tells how his grandmother gave him a Bible with her favorite texts written on the flyleaf. "Among these," he says, "was 'Thou shalt not follow a multitude to do evil.'" Russell adds that "Her emphasis upon this text led me in later life to be not afraid of belonging to small minorities." Throughout his life Russell was a rebel and a champion of unpopular causes. A skeptic, agnostic and pacifist, he became a polemicist late in life, went to jail for his opposition to nuclear weapons and aroused considerable antagonism for his activity in the Ban-the-Bomb movement, his anti-Americanism and his opposition to the Vietnam war.

The greatest single influence on the Athenian general and statesman Pericles was the philosopher Anaxagoras. Anaxagoras, who was only a few years older than Pericles, believed in following knowledge wherever it led him. (He had almost been put to death for insisting after a meteor fell that the sun must be a white-hot stone.)

Both Plato and Plutarch commented in their writings on the powerful effect the philosopher's thinking had on the politician. Plato said that Pericles learned his "elevation of mind and scientific temper" from Anaxagoras, and Plutarch related how Anaxagoras furnished Pericles "most es-

Learning the rules of the game is part of growing up for the little girl in the sequence at right whose eagerness to win makes her peek at the cards held by her friend. Called to task by a fellow card player, she is told that she must stop cheating or be excluded from the game.

pecially with a weight and grandeur of sense, superior to all arts of popularity, and in general gave him his elevation and sublimity of purpose and of character." So great was Anaxagoras' influence, said Plutarch, that Pericles even modeled his "composure of countenance, and a serenity and calmness in all his movements" after him. In Pericles' Athens the highest value was intelligence, and there seems little doubt that the influence of Anaxagoras was decisive in making it so.

The transmission of society's values may be a part of a large organized effort on the part of society itself or one of its instruments. For example, in China before the Communists took over, the family was the basic and most revered institution. In no other large country, perhaps, did the population in general take so much pride in maintaining genealogical records or claim to trace them so far back. Chinese names themselves indicate the importance of the concept of family: of the three characters usually making up a name, the one designating the family is written and spoken first, the second frequently identifies all the cousins of the same generation. The third is the given name. Thus, in the Chinese name the family was exalted rather than the individual.

In pre-Communist China children learned that concept of pride in family early and by a variety of ways. One of the most striking was simple recitation and repetition; children traditionally would begin the day by reciting the names of the hundred most popular families in China. In that way they became aware of the importance of the leading families.

Today, in Communist China, the family has been downgraded in importance, and children no longer memorize prominent family names. But many Chinese living abroad, in cities such as Hong Kong, still emphasize the importance of the family and guard the funeral urns containing ashes of members of their family in temporary resting places for years, awaiting the day when they can return to mainland China and deposit them in their final resting place—their village or ancestral home.

The values and traditions that are esteemed in various societies vary greatly, of course, from one part of the world to the next. Even in societies that are close to each other geographically and would seem, on the surface, to be much alike, the differences may be great, with decisive effects on the upbringing of the children and the lives of all of the societies' members. This can be seen by comparing a pair of island communities in the South Pacific. Both are in Micronesia and their environments and living conditions would seem to be much the same. Yet in crucial ways the attitudes of these societies are strikingly different.

The first of these communities is Palau, in the Caroline Islands. A basic belief here is that people are not to be trusted and hence it is better not to cultivate emotional entanglements. If a child is to survive on Palau, he must learn this attitude early in life. He learns it through a brutal form of conditioning. At the age of five the child, who has been treated with affection up to this point, finds himself suddenly rejected without any explanation. Whereas when he had cried in the past someone would try to

soothe him, now, no matter how prolonged the crying, how wild the temper tantrum, no one, including his mother, pays any attention to him.

This callous treatment is described in *Culture in Process*, a survey of anthropological studies by Alan R. Beals. Anthropologist Homer Barnett, who contributed to the survey, describes the experience of a five-year-old named Azu. As Barnett depicts the scene, the boy is walking along with his mother, tugging at her skirt, because he wants to be carried. He shouts at his mother, but she pays no attention.

"She has resolved not to submit to his plea, for it is time for him to begin to grow up. Azu is not aware that the decision has been made. Understandably, he supposes that his mother is just cross, as she often has been in the past, and that his cries will soon take effect. He persists in his demand, but falls behind as his mother firmly marches on. He runs to catch up and angrily yanks at her hand. She shakes him off without speaking to him or looking at him. Enraged, he drops solidly on the ground and begins to scream. He gives a startled look when this produces no response, then rolls over on his stomach and begins to writhe, sob and yell. He beats the earth with his fists and kicks it with his toes. This hurts and makes him furious, the more so since it has not caused his mother to notice him. He scrambles to his feet and scampers after her, his nose running, tears coursing down his cheeks. When almost on her heel, he yells and, getting no response, drops to the ground."

Azu grovels, squirms and writhes, but his mother still pays him no attention. Other villagers pass by, and they also ignore the boy. He is learning his first lesson in growing up in Palauan society. The experience will be repeated until he finally has learned to accept the Palauan attitude that emotional attachments are to be avoided.

On the tiny atoll of Ulithi, also in the Caroline Islands, a permissive attitude toward child raising prevails and it never really comes to an end as the child matures. A youngster is permitted to suckle up to the age of seven or eight if he wants to, and even at that late date punishment is never used to wean him. Instead, he finally learns by imitating other boys that it is time to give up nursing.

Anthropologists who have studied adults in both Palau and Ulithi have suggested that these learning experiences may have lifelong effects. They have reported that Palauans display anxiety and hostility in social situations. In contrast, the Ulithians are a cheerful people whose lives are filled with laughter and singing.

Even such universal concepts as time and space are subject to varying cultural interpretations. The prevailing method of reckoning time is absorbed by the individual almost from the moment he is born. In busy technological societies where daily activities are tightly scheduled and productivity is valued, time is divided into hours, minutes and seconds, and clock-watching is commonplace. The child who misses the school bus by a couple of minutes may learn a lesson that lasts a lifetime. Years later, conditioned by the experience, he may find himself nervously glancing at his watch and wondering whether he has time for a drink before his commuter train pulls out of the station.

In many nontechnological societies, time is organized on a different scale. The Eskimos, for example, do not break time down into hours, minutes and seconds; there is nothing in their lives that requires the handling of time in such an urgent fashion. Instead their division of time is dictated by what, for them, are more important imperatives—when the seasons change, when animals migrate, when birds nest, when fish spawn, when the ice recedes—all things they need to know to do their work. An Eskimo child, with no reason to learn time in units that are ticked off by a clock, learns instead to measure time by observing and imitating his parents as they go about tasks that change as natural physical cycles change.

The concept of space, like that of time, exists in all cultures, but again the way the concept is organized and the way directions within space are indicated may differ. In complex technological societies directions are denoted by such words as left, right, north and south. Space itself is divided into measurable units: miles, meters, quarts and so on. If space were not organized this way, people would have difficulty performing their routine activities, to say nothing of flying to the moon.

In less sophisticated societies directions may be expressed very differently. To take an extreme example, the Tikopia, a Polynesian people, live on an island in the South Pacific that is so small that they are almost never out of sight or sound of the ocean. According to an anthropologist who has spent some time there, the Tikopians find it almost impossible to conceive of any really large land mass. As a result, in all their references to spatial relationships they use only two expressions: "inland" and "seaward." All objects in their houses are pointed out that way, and on one occasion the anthropologist heard an islander say to another: "There is a spot of mud on your seaward cheek."

While culture plays a crucial role in determining what people learn, the values and beliefs that culture impresses upon its peoples may change drastically under the pressure of outside influences. This effect was observed by anthropologist Margaret Mead in two widely separated visits with the Manus tribe in the Admiralty Islands of the South Pacific. On her first trip there in 1928, she found the Manus "a mere two thousand nearly naked savages, living in pile dwellings in the sea, their earlobes weighed down with shells, their hands still ready to use spears, their anger implemented with magical curses, their morality dependent upon the ghosts of the recently dead." The islanders were "a people without history, without any theory of how they came to be, without any belief in a permanent future life, without any knowledge of geography, without writing, without political forms sufficient to unite more than two or three hundred people."

Twenty-five years later, in 1953, Mead went back to visit the same people to see what had happened to them in the interim. What had happened was the American Army; more than a million men had poured through the Admiralty Islands during World War II bringing with them a highly technological culture. The Americans erected sawmills, built barracks, leveled mountains, hacked out airstrips; the Manus men worked with them —for wages—thus making and handling money for the first time. Equally important in terms of its impact on the Manus was the fact that the Americans apparently had treated them as individuals, not "natives."

What Mead found upon her return in 1953 was a different people entirely. They wore Western-style clothes, lived in Western-style dwellings. They had built a school and hired a local teacher, a man who had been a babe-in-arms when Mead first visited the tribe. They had an elected council and one of the members asked her to help work out a list of rules for modern child care. In short, Mead found they had become "potential members of the modern world, with ideas of boundaries in time and space, responsibility to God, enthusiasm for law, and committed to trying to build a democratic community, educate their children, police and landscape their village, care for the old and the sick, and erase age-old hostilities between neighboring tribes."

In small, homogeneous societies like those of the Manus tribe or the Kpelle farmers, values, traditions and beliefs usually are uniform, and the learning experience of everyone is much the same. But in larger, more intricate societies, a more complex situation prevails. People are affected

Hoisting a wooden glove on a pole at the Honiton, Devon, fair, town crier Tom Lake reenacts a 13th Century ceremony. A symbol of evenhandedness, the glove meant Royal protection for merchants living outside the community. Normally barred by guild laws, they were permitted to trade in town during the fair.

Traditions that unite a people

Tradition is a glue that binds societies together, and no people are more effectively bound by its ties than are the British. All over Britain, from London to the smallest hamlet, hundreds of ceremonies, festivals and pageants are celebrated each year. Englishmen at all levels are involved, with the Queen herself setting the pace by riding out to review the guards every year, on her official birthday, resplendent in scarlet tunic and tricorne hat.

The celebration of traditions on a more humble scale, in English towns and villages, sometimes takes eccentric forms. In Somerset, for example, townspeople sing incantations to the largest apple tree to exorcise evil spirits that might harm the coming crop. Some of the odd observances are shown on these pages. Strange as they may seem, they serve some serious purposes. They give people a chance to share a sense of belonging to the community, to have some fun and to associate themselves firmly with their culture and its past.

Mock mayor of Abingdon, Berkshire,
74-year-old Charlie Brett is chaired down
Ock Street in full regalia by neighbors
who have just elected him to the post.
The ceremony traces its origin to the 15th
Century, when young people selected a
leader for their May Day games. Today,
the mock mayor presides over charity
affairs and neighborhood flower shows.

The task of driving evil spirits out of Bacup, Lancashire, is tackled with verve each Easter Monday by the "Nutters," a group of folk dancers in colorful costumes and wooden clogs. Their blackened faces reflect the origins of the dance, which may have been imported from Moorish-influenced areas of Europe during the Hundred Years' War.

With festoons of spring flowers over his period costume, a Castleton townsman dressed as Charles II is led on horseback to the Garland Day parade. The observance—held each May to celebrate the restoration in 1660 of the Stuart king, who recruited his army in this part of Derbyshire—is a joyous reminder of England's ties to the monarchy. Participants make frequent stops at pubs for fellowship and good cheer and finally deposit the King's Garland at the local church to be on view for all to see.

not only by the culture of the society as a whole but by smaller, independent cultures or subcultures that have a decisive effect on the learning experience of the individual.

India of pre-independence days was a country composed of many cultures and subcultures. Indian society at large was divided into four major castes, or subcultures, plus one other group that comprised the largest subculture of all. First came the Brahmins, or priests and intellectuals; then the Kshatriyas, who were the aristocrats and warriors; the Vaisyas, who included merchants and farmers, and finally the Shudras, who were mostly menial laborers. Membership in a caste was the central fact of Indian life. Each caste had its own status, rules and customs, to be learned and adhered to with the strictest formality. Outside the caste system were 65 million Untouchables, members of one of the most extreme subcultures the world has ever known. For the outcast, the principal reality and the central learning experience of life was the reality of his place at the bottom of Indian society.

What it meant to be an Untouchable is related in a book called *India's Ex-Untouchables* by Harold Isaacs. "In some places they could not contaminate the earth with their spittle but had to carry little pots around their necks to keep the ground reserved for caste Hindu spittle only," Isaacs says. "By some rules an Untouchable had to shout a warning before entering a street so that all the holier folk could get out of the way of his contaminating shadow. By others he could not raise his voice at all because the sound of his voice falling on a caste Hindu's ear was deemed to be as polluting as his touch. Some rules fixed the manner of house he could live in, the style of dress or undress he had to use—in some parts of South India until well past the middle of the nineteenth century, Untouchable women could not wear any clothes above the waist, and in some places even today nothing resembling ornament or finery is allowed. In many areas Untouchables could not have music at their own private festivals, such as weddings. They could not enter any Hindu temple, caste Hindu house, or other establishment, or take water from the common village well. The Untouchables, cut out of the Community altogether, served and largely still do serve—as scavengers and sweepers, the handlers of the carcasses of its dead animals whose flesh they eat, and whose skins they tan, the carriers of waste and night soil, the beggars and the scrapers, living in and off the carrion of the society."

Untouchability was outlawed in India in 1955. But the practice persists in many parts of the country, and caste discrimination is still a major fact of Indian life.

Subcultures and separate cultures, of course, have existed not only in India, but every part of the world; islands of Basques in Spain, Flemish and Walloons in Belgium, and overseas Chinese in Hong Kong—small worlds of peoples, clinging to their own traditions, customs and beliefs, and exerting on their children a stronger learning and behavior influence than any other factor in life. The United States, as the melting pot of peo-

Clad in black hats and coats, and shielding their revered rabbi from the elements with an umbrella, Hasidic Jews in pre-War Mukachevo, Czechoslovakia, personify the power of culture as a learning force. These tightly knit people clung to their traditions, ignoring the outside world. But when Hitler came, the outside world intruded and all but the rabbi and two others were killed.

ples from Europe, Africa and Asia, is a nation forged out of social, racial, ethnic and economic subcultures. Today, under the impact of mass communications, auto and air travel, the country is becoming more and more homogeneous, but the flavor and impact of subcultures can still be strongly felt. And for many Americans the decisive fact of life, in so far as learning and behavior are concerned, has been membership in a particular subculture.

Among the many American subcultures, one of the most distinctive is what is known as High Society, a select group of people whose tribal rites are perhaps as strange as any in the Western world. To be born into this rarefied atmosphere has meant to be committed to learning and observing a set of attitudes and forms of behavior that are almost as carefully prescribed as those in a Benedictine monastery.

The special quality of this subculture is described by Stephen Birmingham in *The Right People*. Birmingham calls it the Real Society. "An Englishman who has made a hobby of studying American Society," he says, "feels that Real Society people are indeed different from you and me. 'You can spot them immediately,' he notes; 'They have a special way of talking, a special way of thinking, and a special look. They even smell a special way.' "

The child who is born into Real Society learns his special place in life by going to the "right" schools, the right dancing classes and the right clubs and associating with the right people. He learns to dress like his fellow Real Society members, talk like them and think like them.

No detail of behavior is too trivial to be learned. "Never point," a San Francisco matron says, "except at French pastry." The lady is explaining proper behavior to her children, who must learn a catalogue of do's and don'ts before they can take their places in Real Society. A mink stole in the daytime is out. Wine must be served *with* meals—and not a California wine either. Food must never be ordinary. "Steak is for butchers," one woman has said.

What it was like to grow up at the opposite end of the special spectrum in America is related by Alfred Kazin in *A Walker in the City*. Kazin lived in a part of Brooklyn called Brownsville, which in the late 19th and early 20th centuries was a gathering place for poor Eastern European Jews fleeing the pogroms and the repression of the Old Country and hoping to find a better life for themselves and their children.

Kazin's book reveals more about the role of a particular subculture in learning than a host of psychological tests. One of the most important values to be learned in Brownsville, he says, was the importance of learning itself. As the parents in that community saw it, learning was the key to the new and better life.

"I was the first American child," he writes; therefore he was his parents' "offering to the strange new God; I was to be the monument of their liberation from the shame of being what they were. . . . It was not for myself alone that I was expected to shine, but for them—to redeem the constant anxiety of their existence." Hence, the first priority was to do well at school. A gold sign above the stage in the great assembly hall trumpeted "KNOWLEDGE IS POWER." A strange new language—English—had to be learned and, because it was "peculiarly the ladder of advancement," it had to be "bright and clean and polished. We were expected to show it off like a new pair of shoes."

Kazin recalls the glee "with which our parents greeted every fresh victory in our savage competition for 'high averages,' for prizes, for a few condescending words of official praise from the principal at assembly" and "the mothers who waited on the stoops every day after three for us to bring home tales of our daily triumphs." Through it all, he says, "it was never learning I associated with that school: only the necessity to succeed, to get ahead of the others in the daily struggle to 'make a good impression.' " Kazin recalls that "All teachers were to be respected like Gods, and God Himself was the greatest of all school superintendents." In the Kazin kitchen, as in all Jewish kitchens in those days, were coin boxes:

"one of these was for the poor, the other to buy back the Land of Israel." He remembered to drop coins in the boxes on the "dreaded morning of 'midterms' and final examinations," Kazin says, "because my mother thought it would bring me luck."

The alternative to not doing well at school was "going bad," Kazin writes, "and the dangers of 'going bad' were constantly impressed upon me at home and in school in dark whispers of the 'reform school.' The effect was traumatic. Anything less than absolute perfection in school always suggested to my mind that I might fall out of the daily race, be kept back in the working class forever, or—dared I think of it?—fall into the criminal class itself."

In that intense no-nonsense atmosphere all idle enjoyment was a sin—especially during the daylight hours. "The daylight was for grimness and labor." Even today Kazin can recall "the bitter guilt" he always felt when he went to the motion pictures in the daytime.

The daily lessons impressed upon the Brownsville children reflected the galling experiences of their parents in the Old Country. The elders had known hunger there; the children would never repeat the experience if their parents could help it. "I can still see," Kazin writes, "the kids pinned down to the tenement stoops, their feet helplessly kicking at the pots and pans lined up before them, their mouths pressed open with a spoon while the great meals are rammed down their throats. *'Eat! Eat! May you be destroyed if you don't eat! What sin have I committed that God should punish me with you! Eat! What will become of you if you don't eat! Imp of darkness, may you sink ten fathoms into the earth if you don't eat! Eat!'*"

When the children came home from school, they would always be nibbling at something (in Yiddish, it is called *noshen*). All a child had to do was call upstairs from the street and there would be flung to him—or lowered on a clothesline—thick slices of rye bread smeared with chicken fat.

What strikes the reader of Kazin's book above all is the strict limits of the particular world he lived in, the perimeters of life that were expected to be learned and accepted by everyone who lived there. There was "The Block" he lived on and the school; everything else was "beyond." Beyond were the "alrightniks"—middle-class Jews who didn't live in Brownsville and were already making out "all right" in the New World. Beyond were the Italians, the Poles, the blacks, all of them to be feared or avoided. Beyond, finally, was New York, the Gentiles. "It was always *them* and us, Gentiles and us, *alrightniks* and us." Everything Alfred Kazin learned as a child and youth in Brownsville was shaped by that alien narrow culture.

Alfred Kazin finally learned enough to escape his subculture and become one of the most respected critics and teachers of literature in the United States. But values he learned as a child—the overriding importance of an education and intellectual pursuits—undoubtedly were a major influence in his adult life.

The contrasts between the members of Real Society and the Brownsville Jews, the Kpelle and the Peace Corps volunteers, the Palauans and the

A second emancipation through learning

One of the most ambitious attempts to indoctrinate people in a culture occurred in the U.S. at the end of the Civil War in 1865. At that point the country faced the problem of educating 4.5 million slaves for places in a society that previously had excluded them. A young teacher named Samuel Chapman Armstrong believed the answer was "to train selected Negro youth who should go out and teach and lead their people."

Accordingly, Armstrong established Hampton Institute at Hampton, Virginia, where hundreds of blacks of both sexes were given three-year courses in agriculture, mechanical arts and domestic sciences. Many of the Hampton graduates became teachers, and one—a young man named Booker T. Washington—founded another famous university, Tuskegee Institute in Alabama.

Applying skills they will later teach,
carpentry students build stairs in
the treasurer's house at Hampton. Much
of the campus was built by students.

Agriculture. Plant life. Study of plants or a "plant society."

Students in a horticulture class learn to
care for greenhouse plants. Surplus U.S.
Army cavalry uniforms were worn
by male students in the postwar years.

Though primarily an industrial school,
Hampton also taught literature,
history and art. Here a geography class
learns about cathedrals in Europe.

Geography. Studying the cathedral towns.

Frances B. Johnston. Photographer. Three plates from an album of Hampton Institute. 1899-1900. Collection, The Museum of Modern Art, New York.

Ulithians are so great as to suggest that mental processes must differ from one society to the next. Otherwise, how could people be committed to such strikingly different attitudes, customs and beliefs? The conclusion that most Western minds would have leaped to 50 or so years ago—that the mental processes of the Pygmies and the Kpelle, "primitive" peoples, are different from and inferior to those of more sophisticated cultures—is unwarranted. Children in out-of-the-way areas of Australia and Micronesia, when given the opportunity, have demonstrated learning capacities on a par with those of other children. Cole and Scribner have reported that in Senegal, school children of the Wolof tribe, when tested on concept making, performed more like Boston school children than like their compatriots who had not been to school.

Another reason for disbelieving the "primitive mind" theory of cultural differences is language. People in all parts of the world learn languages, and even in the most primitive places languages are not simple. The ability to speak and understand any language requires an impressive capacity for abstract thought.

The consensus among social scientists nowadays is that it is culture itself that determines the difference in people's ways of thinking. The key point is that different cultures stimulate the intellect differently, encouraging the individual to develop the processes that are needed to survive in his society. Jerome Bruner, a leading American authority on learning and intellectual processes, who has studied psychological data from various cultures, has concluded that "some environments 'push' cognitive growth better, earlier and longer than others," and that different cultures produce different ways of thinking.

Cole and Scribner, on the basis of their studies, have put it this way: "There is no evidence, in any line of investigation that we have reviewed, that any cultural group wholly lacks a basic process such as abstraction, or inferential reasoning, or categorization."

The common findings among the investigators, say Cole and Scribner, seem to suggest that the sequences in the development of children's learning abilities "are the same from culture to culture." But the *rate* of that development (measured by the age at which children move into the various stages) "has also been consistently found to be slower for non-Western cultures, suggesting a strong influence of culture and environmental factors." Culture may not only determine what people learn, it may also determine the ways their minds work.

This conclusion is supported by the great learning pioneer Jean Piaget, who has suggested that the "final" stage of his four-stage process of conceptual development might not occur at all, or might occur only in a limited form, in nontechnical cultures. In Western cultures this stage covers roughly the teen-age years during which the youth learns to handle and master abstract concepts and propositional thinking. "It is quite possible," Piaget has written, "that in numerous cultures, adult thinking does not proceed beyond the level of *concrete operations*," meaning that it does not develop to the level of abstract thought.

The evidence, of course, does not lend itself to positive, scientific proof. The task of testing and evaluating people all around the world is enormous. But most psychologists believe they have learned enough from their field experiments to lay to rest the myth that people in underdeveloped countries are endowed with primitive mentalities. As George A. Miller, a former president of the American Psychological Association, sums it up: "Every culture has its myths. One of our most persistent is that nonliterate people in less developed countries possess something we like to call a 'primitive mentality' that is both different from and inferior to our own. This myth has it that the 'primitive mind' is highly concrete, whereas the 'Western mind' is highly abstract." The myth also holds, says Miller, that the primitive mind is childish and emotional, able to make connections only by rote association, while the Western mind is "logical and strives to attain consistency."

All of this, he says, is a "hodgepodge of half truths." The truth, he adds, would seem to be that "evolution has not created two different human minds—one for Westerners, another for everybody else. It is culture that develops certain potentials of the human mind here and others there."

Values–the lessons of society

Every society has its values or deeply held beliefs that set it apart from the rest of the world. Some are variations of universal themes; respect for authority, for instance, is a value that is taught everywhere, but the application of this principle varies from one society to the next. In Japan a mother nudges her child to bow to the teacher when they meet on the street, while in India a child is taught to show respect by touching the feet of his elders.

Some values are special to particular societies. The Navaho Indians in America, for example, venerate their ancestors, and therefore elderly people are revered because they are closest to the tribal forebears. On the other hand, the Nyakyusa, an agricultural people of Tanzania, believe so firmly that wisdom resides in their contemporaries that they live in communities made up of individuals of the same age groups.

Children learn their culture's standards from parents, other adults and peers. In some cases they absorb traditional values by taking part in formal rituals like the Catholic confirmation or the bar mitzvah ceremony at which a 13-year-old boy assumes the responsibilities of Judaism.

As the child matures, new experience may cause him to alter his values. A survey of American high school seniors showed that 76 per cent shared their father's political values, but another study shows that the figure drops to between 50 and 60 per cent among college students. This sense of alienation often brings young people of this age group into conflict with society—which helps explain why in the 1960s and 1970s students of a dozen nations rioted against their governments' policies.

Important social values are often identified with well-known figures. Here, at a 1967 news conference, a little girl listens to civil rights leader Martin Luther King Jr., whose fight for social justice made him a symbol of this ideal.

Precepts conveyed from generation to generation

Transmitting religious values, a father in Peru, whose population is 95 per cent Roman Catholic, teaches his children to revere the Virgin Mary, and to imitate her virtues, in hope of salvation.

Inculcating patriotism, a father watches a parade in New York City with his two sons. The flag and buttons he has bought for them serve to reinforce his lesson.

Learning the code of the group

Scrupulously playing by the rules, youngsters on an island off South Carolina compete at marbles. From such peer groups the child learns to accept the value of reasonable regulation in life.

Everybody on the same side pulls together as these French Cub Scouts play tug of war at a jamboree in Paris. Such teamwork begins around age seven, experts say, but is sporadic till 11 or 12.

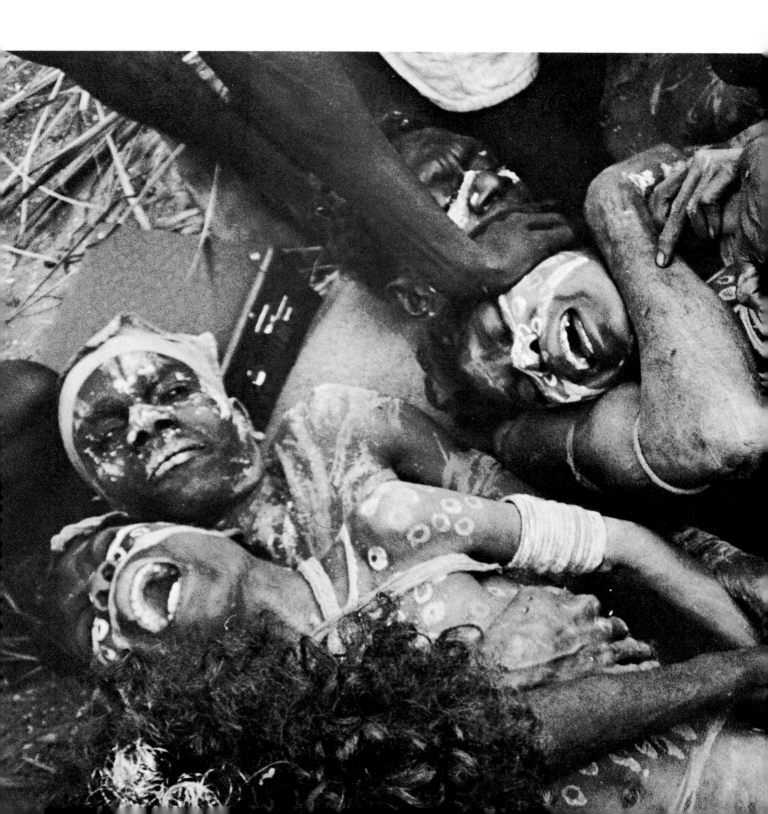

Lying supine atop their guardians, two young Australian aborigines scream in pain as they are circumcised at the climax of a weeks-long ritual that ushers them into manhood. The ordeal symbolizes their separation from childhood dependence upon their mothers and their introduction to values such as physical courage that the tribe expects of its men.

Carrying on the custom of the land

Having learned that society cherishes life and mourns its passing, a little girl conducts a funeral for her pet mouse, complete with miniature coffin and flowers as an expression of the grief she feels.

In Southeastern Asia, children are taught the value of looking after their younger siblings. Here two eight-year-olds in Hong Kong carry on the tradition, their brothers securely tied to their backs.

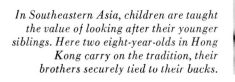

Making a choice when ideals conflict

*Clinging to her youth, a sunbather in
Nice, France, wears a bikini in preference
to more conservative attire usually
adopted by people as they become older.*

*Burning his draft card during an anti-
Vietnam War demonstration at the
Pentagon, a young man chooses the value
of following his own conscience over
that of fighting in his country's service.*

The Changing Classroom

6

Few topics cause people more concern, or fray their tempers more readily, than the education their children get in school. The concern is worldwide. In 1974, Japan was embroiled in a heated nationwide debate over some changes in educational procedure—such as playing the national anthem in schools and teaching a long-abandoned ethics course—that had been demanded by conservatives. The ethics course especially alarmed some Japanese, for its basic message seemed to glorify unduly an older, more nationalistic and militaristic Japan, reawakening attitudes that led to the country's catastrophic involvement in World War II; many parents did not want their children exposed to what were in their view outmoded and even dangerous ideas.

In Britain arguments over educational shortcomings have flared up almost constantly since World War II, and in West Germany proposed school reform became a hot election issue in 1974. Italy has also endured a high-pitched battle over the quality of education offered by its system. Soviet leaders have pushed for decades to change the emphasis of Russian education, hoping to direct into industrial careers increasing numbers of bright children like the Moscow pupils eagerly exercising at left. The United States, for its part, seems to be in continual turmoil over the quality of education. In the late 1960s, students in one institution after another across the country were in a state of revolt over what they considered to be the inadequacies of the kind of schooling offered them. Parents and teachers carry on running debates over the merits of one system or another, while government reports assess, alternately with alarm and satisfaction, the state of the nation's schools.

It is little wonder that the organized process of learning in schools calls forth such passions. Every parent is naturally and deeply concerned about the way his children are prepared for life—what knowledge and skills they acquire. Although much learning goes on outside the school, especially in the home during the early childhood years, the school is a crucial arena. It is where most formal learning occurs, where children develop such necessary skills as reading and mathematical computation, where they learn the rudiments of science and become aware of their cultures and traditions through the study of literature and history.

The debate about what and how children should be taught in school has

been going on a long time. It puzzled even the incisive mind of Aristotle. He did not know, he said some 2,400 years ago, what things the "young ought to learn, either with a view to virtue or with a view to the best life, nor is it clear whether their studies should be regulated more with regard to intellect or with regard to character."

A variant of this argument has arisen in modern Britain, among other places. Some Englishmen maintain that only the gifted young should receive an edifying liberal arts education while the less gifted should get practical, useful instructions for a trade. Other English citizens heatedly maintain that every child should have a chance at a full liberal-arts program. Similar controversies have recently troubled France and Germany, where traditionally only a select few have been prepared for university training and the prize careers it brings.

Perhaps even more puzzling has been the question of how a child learns best whatever it is that the school tries to teach him. Everybody has agreed in all civilized nations going back to ancient Athens that education is of great importance to the state and to individuals, but few have agreed how that education should be provided. Does a child learn best if facts are crammed into his memory by practice and repetition? Or does a less rigid approach, in which the teacher tries to engage the child's natural curiosity, work better? Certain kinds of learning simply have to be memorized —the multiplication tables, for example, and the rules of spelling. Rote memory must play some role in education, and repetitive drill seems to be the best way to affix certain kinds of information in the student's mind. Does this mean, however, that most sorts of learning can, or should, be taught in the same way? Should learning be fun for the student, or is schooling necessarily such hard work that the child must be forced to do it? And then there is the practical problem: How can a teacher with a class of, say,

40 students take the time to make things fun, to coax and cajole the slower children into learning what needs to be learned?

These questions have rung down through the centuries, but they have gained added importance in modern times as schooling has been extended around the world to every child, regardless of his background, his desires, even occasionally of his intellectual capacity. Not very long ago school education, where it existed, was limited to the aristocracy and the wealthy. But during the 19th Century one nation after another—Germany, France, England, the United States and others—built vast systems of schools offering free education to every child. The three-level system became the civilized standard; a primary or grade school, then some form of secondary school education available to all, with a third level, college or university, for the gifted. In this century the ideal of a basic education for every child has spread to Russia, the Orient and to other nations everywhere. Virtually every country has subscribed to the United Nations Declaration of Human Rights, which calls upon member nations to offer at least a primary education to all children, free.

These announced intentions to provide an education for everyone are of course laudable, but they serve also to focus attention on actual performance, on the numbers of children of school age who are being educated and on the quality of the education they are getting. And the lamentable fact is that despite great concern for education, and despite the expenditure of large sums of money on nationwide school systems, too many children are not being educated at all or are not being educated properly.

In Italy only one boy out of five graduates from secondary school. Critics claim teachers do not teach well enough or hard enough to reach the slower students, who therefore either drop out or fail and are expelled. The teachers reply that it is not their job to coddle stupid students, that the ones who failed were ineducable to start with.

The United States has compulsory education to the age of 16, but the quality of the education leaves much to be desired. A recent survey estimated that one fifth of all the citizens of the country could not comprehend the contents of a good newspaper. The problem of low-quality education has been stated succinctly by John Holt, a teacher and school critic, in his book, *How Children Fail*. Holt says that many American high school students get their diplomas only because "we have agreed to push them up through the grades and out of the schools, whether they know anything or not." Even the good students, he adds, "fail to develop more than a tiny part of the tremendous capacity for learning, understanding, and creating with which they were born and of which they made full use during the first two or three years of their lives."

The major fault pinpointed by Holt is a simple one that is very difficult to remedy: Too many schools—even supposedly very good ones—inculcate in students not a joy in learning but an intellectually paralyzing fear of failure. These children suffer every day in school; they are afraid they will give a wrong answer and make fools of themselves before the teacher

and their fellow students. Fear freezes them and prevents them from thinking and getting the right answers. For such students, says Holt, school is little better than a prison: "It is a place where *they* make you go and where *they* tell you to do things and where *they* try to make your life unpleasant if you don't do them or don't do them right. For children, the central business of school is not learning . . . it is getting these daily tasks done, or at least out of the way, with a minimum of effort and unpleasantness."

All too often, Holt charges, school in America is anything but an exciting adventure into new fields of learning. It is rather a succession of meaningless tasks—meaningless because the unstimulated child is unable to see any point in the work assigned him or to understand how one assignment connects with another. He performs his tasks with a kind of dull despair of ever getting them right. Failure breeds further failure and more hopelessness, ad infinitum.

Even more severe judgments than Holt's have been made on the same grounds by psychiatrist William Glasser and critics Jonathan Kozol and Charles Silberman. Glasser says flatly that the general run of the schools in the United States blight the lives of most students instead of achieving the educational objective of making their lives better. Jonathan Kozol's book, which bears the chilling title *Death at an Early Age*, states its conclusion in its subtitle: "The Destruction of the Hearts and Minds of Negro Children in the Boston Public Schools."

Silberman's *Crisis in the Classroom* is a 550-page indictment of American education from top to bottom. Silberman acknowledges that U.S. schools—particularly the colleges and universities—are now vastly superior in equipment and teaching to those of the 19th Century and the first half of the 20th Century. But the improvement has not gone deep enough; grade schools and high schools are especially lacking. Silberman quotes psychologist Erik Erikson: "The most deadly of all possible sins is the mutilation of a child's spirit." And Silberman finds such mutilation all too common. "It is not possible," he says, "to spend any prolonged period visiting public school classrooms without being appalled by the mutilation visible everywhere—mutilation of spontaneity, of joy in learning, of pleasure in creating, of sense of self. . . . Because adults take the schools so much for granted, they fail to appreciate what grim, joyless places most American schools are."

Silberman, Holt and these other writers are Americans, but such scholastic shortcomings are by no means an American monopoly. A bill of particulars against schools in Italy, for example, has been provided in a remarkable book, *Letter to a Teacher*. It was written by eight Italian teenagers, all of whom had been expelled from the regular Italian school system. These eight rejects plus others in the same situation subsequently attended a small informal school set up by a local priest in a tiny northern Italian town called Barbiana. One of their student projects was to research and write their "letter" criticizing the school system that had failed them.

Their main criticisms resemble Holt's. First, the system had ignored the

students who most needed its care and attention—the apparently slower children, the thinkers, the plodders—while rewarding the clever ones who had the knack of pleasing teachers and getting good grades. Second, the Italian secondary schools concentrated only on grades and in moving the children lock step through a required curriculum. The eight boys describe with passion and precision the qualities of students who succeed:

"Day in and day out they study for grades, for report cards and diplomas. Meanwhile they lose interest in all the fine things they are studying. Languages, sciences . . . everything becomes purely grades.

"Behind those sheets of paper there is only a desire for personal gain. The diploma means money. . . . To be a happy student in your schools you have to be a social climber at the age of twelve.

"But few are climbers at twelve. It follows that most of your young people hate school."

The eight Barbiana schoolboy-authors are equally harsh on unimaginative teachers who do not even try to bring out the potential of lagging students. One peasant boy whom they call Gianni was dropped from school. His fate still haunts them. A good teacher, instead of failing Gianni, they say, "would search out . . . the intelligence that God has put in him, as in all children. You would fight for the child who needs you most. . . . You would wake up at night thinking about him and would try to invent new ways to teach him—ways that would fit his needs."

The informal, unofficial school that the boys attended at Barbiana was different. They report that it "did not seem like a school. No teacher, no desk, no blackboard, no benches. Just big tables, around which we studied and also ate." The institution was geared to develop the potential of every student. "There a boy who had no background, who was slow or lazy was made to feel like the favorite. He would be treated the way you teachers treat the best student in the class."

The success of the Barbiana school is eloquently attested by the book itself. It is written in clean, forceful prose, closely reasoned and based on wide research into the Italian school system. And it was written by youths who had been rejected by that system.

The waste of good minds, the frequent failure to develop talents and engage the deep interest of many students, continues despite the money and concern that have gone into efforts to make schools more effective. Sweeping and expensive reforms are attempted and still the dropout rate climbs. Even more tragically, this human loss continues even though the education wisdom of the past and psychological insights of the present show how education can be made more effective. Every person who has ever thought about education agrees that teaching should be more effective than it is, that schools should stimulate every child's mind as well as teach him useful knowledge, that techniques should be invented to reach and educate even the least promising students. Such concern came into focus during the 15th Century, when Renaissance scholars considered ways of teaching children the newly rediscovered knowledge of the ancient world. Surprisingly, the thoughts of these philosophers of centuries past are strikingly similar to the proposals modern psychologists have made for improving the learning process.

A spokesman for the Humanist scholars and teachers of the Renaissance was the Italian Vittorino da Feltre. Vittorino ran a school himself and so realized firsthand that children are far from being alike—in fact, are remarkable for their differences. It was the duty of the teacher, Vittorino wrote, to stretch his mind to find ways to make education enjoyable for his charges. Vittorino called his schoolroom the happy house. He evidently made the name apt, breaking off the Latin lessons when they became too heavy and turning to an interlude of roughhousing with his charges. He preached the enlightened doctrine, forgotten too often by busy teachers, that it is absurd to expect every child to respond the same way at the same time. The teacher, Vittorino said, should carefully study his pupils before asking them to do any studying.

Vittorino's ideas have been rediscovered again and again since his time. In the 16th Century, Michel de Montaigne, the great French essay writer, protested that there were too many inadequate teachers who "stuff the memory and leave the understanding void." To Montaigne, true learning was not memory but thought, not the content of books but understanding. "It is not enough to join learning and knowledge to the mind, it should be incorporated into it; the mind must not be sprinkled but dyed with it." What is wanted, said Montaigne, is wisdom, and the best way to foster the development of wisdom is to make every lesson an occasion for the student to exercise his own judgment.

The need to involve children actively in their own education and make education an enjoyable process was also the essential message of John Amos Comenius, a Czech teacher and clergyman of the following century. A kind and pious man, Comenius lived in the brutal era of the Thirty Years' War. His home was pillaged twice by marauding troops, his wife and children were killed, and his books and writings were burned. But these catastrophes and the persecution of the religious sect—the Moravian Brethren—of which Comenius became bishop, did not modify his concern for children and their education. He was at least 200 years ahead of his time in insisting that all should be educated—rich or poor, noble or peasant—and that natural science should be taught in school. He even recommended that children should be schooled in their native tongue rather than be force-fed Latin at the expense of everything else. He favored sunny classrooms with pictures on the walls and ample space for play outdoors. And, in an era when most schoolmasters were grimly authoritarian, he wanted bright, cheerful teaching. "Children," he observed, "detest pedantry and severity."

The main points of Comenius' pedagogical theory, however, are more profound than the benefits of cheerful classrooms. Children should not, he said, be shoved through an unrelieved regime of book knowledge and memorization. Rather they should contemplate "the living book of the world instead of dead papers." They should be encouraged to observe the realms of nature and of men directly, asking questions, absorbing information through their senses. They should also learn by doing things. "Artisans learn to forge by forging, to carve by carving," and so "let children learn to write by writing . . . to reason by reasoning." Above all, students should not be loaded with disjointed facts; instead they should be taught how things connect—the principles that govern reality.

The enlightened approach of Comenius was extended a century later by Johann Heinrich Pestalozzi, who, as his German-Italian name suggests, was born in that multilingual European crossroads, Switzerland. Most of Pestalozzi's life was, from a practical point of view, a succession of failures. He started one school after another only to see them successively go under. During the violent years of Napoleon, the tender-hearted Pestalozzi volunteered to teach a group of children who had been orphaned when French troops razed a Swiss town and killed the parents. No sooner had he established his school for orphans, however, than the tides of war changed and French troops poured back into the area, commandeering the school building for a barracks and throwing Pestalozzi and his young charges into the street. But he persevered and finally, when he was almost

Overseeing his radical educational venture, A. S. Neill (right) calmly puffs his pipe as Summerhill students and staff debate policy.

Summerhill's smashing education

The best known, and perhaps the most radical, attempt to let children learn as they please was initiated at Summerhill, a coeducational institution in England, founded in 1924 by a Scottish educator named A. S. Neill. Dismayed by the rigidity of traditional schooling, Neill believed that the purpose of education should be to prepare a child for a happy life, and pupils should be free to pursue their own interests without fear of adult interference or discipline.

Students at Summerhill, who range from five to 16, study whatever they want. Classes are optional—one boy went there for 13 years without ever at-tending a class. Students are encouraged to work out their hostilities; when one new boy started smashing windows, the school's headmaster told him to break as many as he wanted but suggested that he improve his aim.

Since Neill died in 1973, his wife has carried on the freewheeling tradition at Summerhill. Its effectiveness is disputed. When 50 alumni were interviewed in 1965, many complained that Summerhill's academic standards were not high enough. But others reported that they felt they had become personally more tolerant and more individualistic for having gone there.

60, founded a successful school in the Swiss town of Yverdon. The fame of Pestalozzi's teaching eventually spread so widely that several farsighted nations began giving their prospective teachers scholarships to travel to Yverdon and observe Pestalozzi's methods.

Like Comenius, Pestalozzi decried the practice of stuffing children's minds with useless facts; such learning was, he said, "empty chattering." He too thought that every child, boy or girl, rich or poor, should have an education. But he went beyond other theorists in contending that a child's schooling should not be a special experience divorced from the youngster's total experience of growing up. School should instead be part of a living, organic process, drawing on the child's natural interests and abilities to learn. Children on their own are eager to learn, he maintained, but over the ages schools too often had stifled this natural inclination. Education, he said, should be the "natural, progressive, and harmonious development of all the child's powers and faculties."

A German named Friedrich Froebel, who studied Pestalozzi's methods, carried the master's conception of "natural" and "harmonious" development a step further. Froebel's mind was tinged with religious mysticism; he believed that the development of every child, and of every adult for that matter, was ordained by God to be a harmonious part of an evolving universe. To him it was criminal, even blasphemous, for a school to bend the child's individual endowment. The school's job was to help the child develop to the fullest his own spontaneous, creative gifts. Evil occurred when the child, frustrated, betrayed and abandoned, felt he had no choice but to become bitter and rebellious. Froebel said all this in the 1830s, but his statements echo in the late 20th Century.

Although Froebel's theories had a brief vogue, they were soon forgotten, except for one innovation that has flourished to this day—the kindergarten. In 1837 he set up a school for very young children in an abandoned mill in the tiny German village of Blankenburg. Froebel coined a German jawbreaker of a word to describe his experiment; it was a *Kleinkinderbeschäftigungsanstalt,* "an institution where small children are occupied." Then in 1840, a happy inspiration changed the name to a less ponderous and more enduring one: *Kindergarten,* a "garden for children." It exactly conveyed his purpose, to create a place where children could grow as naturally as the flowers in a garden.

Despite all the humane thought, from Vittorino to Pestalozzi and Froebel, that had been lavished on improving education, the schools of the 19th Century remained by and large cheerless jailhouses where teachers pounded lessons into unwilling skulls, often with the aid of rulers, whips or canes. A spokesman for the rigid, no-nonsense schooling of the time was an English educator of the early 19th Century, Samuel Wilderspin, who ran schools for pupils of tender years, from kindergarten through the lower grades. Instead of following Comenius' advice to vary book learning with observation of the world, Wilderspin overwhelmed his young charges with books. He freighted his pupils with cargoes of information—tables of weights and measures, lists of England's exports and imports, scientific facts. This was topped off by uplifting lessons from the New Testament, since Wilderspin (like many pedants) conceived that his young charges were inherently depraved and in need of moral toning up.

It was Wilderspin's sort of school that Charles Dickens attacked with savage humor in his novel *Hard Times*. Dickens' pedant, appropriately named Mr. Gradgrind, announces his teaching program: "Now what I want is Facts. Teach these boys and girls nothing but Facts. Facts alone are wanted in life. Plant nothing else, and root out everything else. . . . In this life, we want nothing but Facts, sir; nothing but Facts!" Gradgrind will not tolerate poetry or music or any other humanizing distraction from his ironclad curriculum. The schoolmaster employed to cram facts into the students at Gradgrind's academy has another wonderful Dickensian name: Mr. McChoakumchild.

Dickens was not alone in attacking shortsighted pedants. An American educational philosopher from Massachusetts named Horace Mann also rose up to battle the Gradgrinds. Mann visited the school systems of several European countries in 1842. He found his notion of the ideal in Prussia. The Prussian educational authorities had sent observers to Yverdon some years before to find out what Pestalozzi was doing. They were so impressed that they adopted Pestalozzi's humane methods for their schools' early grades. Mann found Prussian pupils and teachers in a "beautiful relation of harmony." He "heard no child ridiculed, sneered at, or scolded for making a mistake." He pressed the Massachusetts school authorities to adopt Pestalozzi's methods.

The reaction of those clinging to the old ways was ferocious. To make learning enjoyable, as Mann urged, would destroy all discipline and foster mischief, the Massachusetts Gradgrinds said. Coddling children as Pestalozzi and the Prussians recommended would threaten "the welfare, both of the individual and society, by sending forth a sickly race, palsied in every limb, through idleness." The town fathers of Newburyport, Massachusetts, added that school days "are those emphatically in which the individual is taught obedience. . . . Pupils need governing and this . . . always means coercing, compelling."

Despite such opposition, Mann campaigned hard for his ideas and raised money to build new schools and improve teacher training in Massachusetts. And he influenced the most notable of American school reformers, the philosopher John Dewey. Dewey, like other students of education before him, noted that children will work relentlessly when doing tasks they enjoy, using their minds and in the process learning quickly and well. A 12-year-old who wants a bicycle for his birthday will study catalogues tirelessly and in a day or two master the technical names for every part and know the advantages and defects of every available make. Or a group of children who want to build a clubhouse will quickly scrounge the needed lumber, assemble the required tools and nail together a shack. These

The purposeful chaos of the "open classroom" approach to education is apparent at Finmere in England, where pupils in informal groups exercise, tootle on recorders, play games, paint or read. Dressed as they wish, they select their own classroom activities. Critics of this loose-structured method, pioneered in England, charge that it assumes children know more about education than adults. Proponents argue that it makes children more interested in learning.

may be the same children who seem almost impervious to learning in an uninspiring classroom.

To Dewey this disparity between the child's natural eagerness to learn and the general performance of children in schools was a crime. His answer was what came to be known as the progressive school. In the early grades especially, the child would be encouraged to do things he enjoyed doing—paint, build things, read, study a flower, play a game. Dewey's contention was that the interested child would discover as he played that he needed to learn to read or to write or to add and subtract. He would turn to the teacher for help, of course, but his learning would be almost a by-product of his other interests. Dewey tested his theory by founding an experimental school while he was a professor at the University of Chicago, and other schools around the country adopted his philosophy.

Conservatives fought Dewey's approach, saying that while the children in such schools might be interested and active, they were failing to grasp the rudiments of reading, spelling, and so on. Many of these objections were justified. Dewey himself would have repudiated some of his more extreme disciples, who were so busy making school enjoyable that very little learning of any sort took place. Complete permissiveness, it became clear, is not education. Children need—in fact, want—to be guided, and some sorts of information must still be drilled into them.

There may never be a clear resolution of the conflict between the advocates of Dewey's progressive schools and the conservatives who insist on authoritative training. Both systems can work, but they work differently, the results varying with the social milieu and with educational goals.

The efficacy of a rigid curriculum of intellectual studies in an authoritarian setting would seem to be demonstrated by at least one nationwide school system—that of France. Every school in France must follow to the letter the course of study fixed by the central authority in Paris. Serious work begins when the child enters school at age six and continues at least until age 16, with stiff examinations testing proficiency at the end of every year. The curriculum has no frills—it consists of French language and literature, a second modern language, history, mathematics—and it is taught by well-trained teachers who brook no nonsense. A French school circular dated 1882 defines the aim: "The primary school's ideal is not to teach a great deal, but to teach it well. Children leave school with a limited knowledge, but what they have been taught they know thoroughly." Anybody who knows France and the French realizes that this aim is often achieved. Perhaps no other people know so much about their own or other nations' cultures—or for that matter, can think more clearly or logically.

The French educational system has faults. One is that only about 25 per cent of all French students receive secondary education in a *lycée*. Those who do pay a high price in grindingly hard work; probably no secondary schools anywhere are so intellectually demanding as those of France. French students themselves complain of *bourrage*—"stuffing." But the results again are impressive. At age 18 or 19, when they leave the *lycée*,

A private refuge for study, in striking contrast with the hubbub of the open classroom (pages 146-147), is provided for third-grade pupils at the Avery Coonley School in Downers Grove, Illinois, by special octahedrons perched above the main classroom space. Each of these learning spaces is equipped with its own desk, lamp, fold-up seat and openings through which the teacher can give the pupils special instruction.

French students know considerably more than all but the best trained U.S. college graduates, who are usually at least three years older. At no point in the French educational process do teachers attempt to develop students' personalities—they educate the mind and that is that.

While the success of the rigid French system seems noteworthy, a somewhat similar approach in England has been regarded more equivocally. There the celebrated boarding schools such as Eton, Harrow and Winchester have taught a limited range of subjects—the standard fare is still English, French, Latin, Greek, mathematics and history—and have made sure that their students got a lot of each, especially the Classics, stuffed into their heads. And they have produced some very learned men. But the cost, some critics have said, is too high.

The rigid, almost military discipline of these schools—where corporal punishment for infractions of the rules or classroom laziness used to be the rule—has produced men with what E. M. Forster, the great English novelist, called "undeveloped hearts." As Forster saw it, the stoical, stiff-upper-lip attitude of the British upper classes sometimes indicated not courage but emotional frigidity; the natural wellsprings of joy and human sympathy had too often been dried up, he felt, by the severity of the schooling. And if such schools produced some great scholars as well as poets and novelists, they also produced many men who loathed anything intellectual for the rest of their lives.

Severest of the critics of this system, perhaps, was English writer George Orwell, who, in an essay ironically titled "Such, Such Were the Joys," pictures English boarding-school life as a time of almost unrelieved cruelty and desolation. The teachers hammered the lessons into Orwell and his classmates with tireless ferocity and whipped them when they made errors. They did learn, but, Orwell says, they did not really learn well. Even the prized subjects, Latin and Greek, "were deliberately taught in a flashy, unsound way. We never, for example, read right through even a single book of a Greek or Latin author: we merely read short passages which were picked out because they were the kind of thing likely to be set as an 'unseen translation,'" that is, they might well be included in an examination. "It is a mistake," Orwell goes on, "to think such methods"—endless repetitions and occasional beatings—"do not work. They work very well for their special purpose,"—to cram examination-passing information into children's heads and sometimes to give a simulacrum of knowledge rather than true learning.

In the 1960s and early 1970s evidence began piling up that the schools in several countries were combining the worst of both approaches—teaching was unimaginative and rigid, and yet little knowledge was being imparted. In the United States attacks on educational shortcomings became particularly sharp. Some said the entire system was so rotten, so full of bad teaching, ironclad curricula, stupid rules and other evils, that there was no choice but to scrap the entire structure and start again. Silberman's *Crisis in the Classroom,* which summarized the feelings of many observers

Seated at a computerized "talking typewriter" a little boy learns to read and spell. As a picture flashes on the screen above him, the machine's voice identifies the image and helps the child spell the word on the keyboard. Such teaching machines supplement the work of books and teachers but are no substitute.

that the schools by and large were restrictive and boring, helped to set in motion a number of new approaches to the management of learning.

Silberman characterized the deadening rigidity of most schools in the United States, and other nations as well, with two incidents. In the first, a visitor to a supposedly good school sees a cluster of excited children "examining a turtle with enormous fascination and intensity. 'Now, children, put away the turtle,' the teacher insists. 'We're going to have our science lesson.' The lesson is on crabs." In another vignette Silberman makes the point even more clearly. During the last week of November 1963, he reported, teachers all over the United States uttered the same complaint: "I can't get the children to concentrate on their work; all they want to do is talk about the assassination." Silberman comments: "The idea that the children might learn more from discussing President Kennedy's assassination —or that like most adults, they were simply too obsessed with the horrible event to think about anything else—simply didn't occur to these teachers. It wasn't in that week's lesson plan."

This rigid approach is reflected in a report made by the Harvard Graduate School of Education after an analysis of the supposedly excellent school system of Watertown, Massachusetts. The findings are summed up as follows: "The student is not encouraged to explore, to stretch his thinking, to pursue an independent line of inquiry. The program of studies is defined by the school, and the student is expected to learn what the school decides he should learn. Rarely does the student in Watertown have the chance to make meaningful decisions; rarely does he have a chance to discover for himself what learning is all about. . . . The emphasis is on the acquisition of factual information untempered by reflective thought."

Plainly, this kind of approach is not going to foster creative thinking. It may force the bright, natural learners to absorb information that they can build on later. But it is going to stultify the student who needs to have his interest and ambition aroused. The question remains, what is the alternative? Is there a way to convey all the learning a child must acquire without turning off his innate interest in the world around him?

The answer the English give is "yes." In Britain since World War II there has been a gradual country-wide changeover in the methods used to educate children in the primary grades. The experiment appears to be a success, indicating that schools can be humane and joyful and still do a good job of educating their students. The record of those schools that have adopted the new methods also suggests that concern for the individual and his fulfillment can be maintained without forgetting intellectual development. These so-called open schools abandoned the previously strict timetable of 50-minute classes followed by most schools and instituted long periods during which, with the teacher's encouragement and direction, children pursue a variety of activities. In a typical class, some paint, others read, still others do a simple experiment demonstrating a physical law, while yet another group rehearses a short play. The teacher does not lecture or spend time keeping order; instead, he circulates among the children helping and advising, drawing the students' attention to new possibilities, new projects. The emphasis is on enticing the child to learn.

The atmosphere in a well-run open school is summed up by an anecdote Silberman tells about a visit by an American teacher. The school is so new that carpenters, painters and electricians are still swarming over the building. The American turns to the British headmistress and says sardonically of the confusion, "You must love that!" "Oh, I do," replies the British headmistress enthusiastically. "The children are fascinated by the workmen, and the workmen are interested in what the children are doing." Silberman comments, "Instead of being considered an intrusion, the workmen have been made part of the learning environment."

The way that the new British schools teach mathematics illustrates how the children are led to acquire learning on their own. The typical schoolroom has tables covered with sand and various shapes for filling—cones, cylinders, cubes, pint bottles and boxes—to impart knowledge of measures and shapes. On another table there may be beads, buttons and pebbles for counting and a scale for weighing, along with blocks and rods that can be used to demonstrate principles of elementary algebra. By age seven the children are expected to have discovered an astonishing lot of mathematics —addition, subtraction, multiplication, division, proportion and ratio.

One unusual mathematics exercise was undertaken by the boys of the primary school of Wallingford, England. The River Thames flows by the school and the teacher posed the question, "How many gallons of water flow under Wallingford Bridge in 24 hours?" First the boys took a ball of string and carried one end across the bridge to the other bank, then got down in the mud by the pilings of the bridge and used the string to measure the river's width. Their teacher then showed them how to check the answer given by the string through the use of triangles—in other words, geometry. They also measured the river's depth. The next task was to determine how fast the river flowed. The technique used was simple: they dropped bottles into the water to see how far they would travel in 15 minutes. The answer was 800 feet. Multiplying by four, they found the river's speed was 3,200 feet per hour, and 24 times that gave them the flow for a day. Then, using the formulas for square and cubic measure, they determined how many gallons passed under the bridge each 24 hours. (The answer was 246 million gallons.) A simple-seeming problem, but the schoolboys had learned through their own experiments a great deal of quite advanced mathematics.

Of course, there are drawbacks to these methods. The children progress unevenly in Britain's new primary schools, some gaining great proficiency, say, in mathematics and less skill in reading, or vice versa. When they get to secondary school at age 11 or 12, they may be excellently prepared in some areas and not so well in others. But according to some British educators, such gaps are unimportant compared with the children's general ability to learn. One Oxfordshire secondary school headmaster, for example, says that he finds children from the new primaries "much more alive—much better able to express themselves, with such enquiring minds and such a good attitude toward education that this is worth any small loss of particular skills."

M uch of the theory behind such attempts to reform educational practice goes back to Comenius, Froebel and Dewey. But it also derives directly from the work done by Jean Piaget. Piaget's great contribution has been to demonstrate that the child learns primarily through his own activity. He forms a concept, broadens the concept by assimilating new information or alters it by accommodating seemingly contradictory evidence. In Piaget's view the child learns best by doing things himself and by thinking for himself, and his own activity is the critical factor.

Piaget emphasizes that children should not merely be loaded down with facts but should be taught to think. If they are going to function effectively in a tormented and confusing world, they must be encouraged to create new ideas and concepts. In Piaget's words: "The principal goal of education is to create men who are capable of doing new things, not simply of repeating what other generations have done. . . . The great danger today is of slogans, collective opinions, ready-made trends of thought. We have to be able to resist individually, to criticize, to distinguish between what is proven and what is not."

Other psychologists have strongly seconded Piaget. One of the most in-

Television, piped to the country's outlying areas from the capital of Niamey, brings a French lesson to pupils in a dirt-floor classroom in Niger.

fluential has been Jerome Bruner, a leader in modern psychology and a prominent theorist on education. Successful teaching, according to Bruner, must promote what he calls the act of discovery. Too much teaching, Bruner believes, depends on the "expository mode." The teacher lectures, while the student passively listens. It is far better, says Bruner, for student and teacher to work together to solve a problem. The student sees the evidence, thinks about it, tries one solution and then another. Finally he arrives at the correct solution, perhaps with some coaching from the teacher, but largely on his own. In this approach, the student does more than acquire facts. He works with the evidence to arrive at conclusions himself. He thus increases his power of logical thought. Further, the act of discovering the answers for himself is exciting.

The insights of educational philosophers from the past and the more recent findings of modern psychologists have borne fruit in the United States as well as in England. School boards in places as distant as New York and North Dakota have tried open classrooms for younger children and have also altered their secondary school curricula, making them more flexible, more concerned with the individual student, more imaginative in both teaching and courses of study. Perhaps the most unusual is Philadelphia's "school without walls," called the Parkway Program. In effect it makes the city of Philadelphia itself the school and the life of the city the curriculum. Students study in the city's offices, museums, hospitals, theaters and department stores. They can opt for such courses as law enforcement and do their own research on the subject in the administration building of Philadelphia's Police Department. They can pursue biology at the local natural history museum. "The purpose," says an advocate of this unique school, "is to show that learning can be acquired without the four-walled boxes called classrooms."

Other schools have achieved impressive results by using the students' interests as a springboard for learning experiences. The Urban League of Greater New York founded Harlem Prep in 1967 in an attempt to educate dropouts from the ordinary schools of the black ghetto. The studies started with what has been called a contact curriculum, which means that the teachers found out what the students already knew and began building from there, instead of trying to teach things wholly unknown and alien to ghetto-raised youths. Once the student was interested—and, for the first time, confident of being able to accomplish something—he could then be led into more adventurous realms. The success in some cases was astounding. Students certified as ineducable by city schools, teenagers who could read only at a level considered appropriate to a 10-year-old, were soon enjoying Plato's dialogues and Sophocles' plays.

In some experimental schools the contact with what students know may lead to a seemingly outlandish learning project. Hot rodding was one choice. How can children be educated this way? John Holt answers the question by pointing out that the hot rod—a remodeled and souped-up automobile—is a machine touching on physics, chemistry, thermodynamics

In the bustling activity of Sesame Street, prominently placed signs provide an important, unspoken, environmental lesson for youngsters.

Learning faster on Sesame Street

Except for the presence of an eight-foot puppet named Big Bird, the scene above might well be a city block almost anywhere in the United States. But in fact it is a set from the award-winning television program *Sesame Street*, one of the brightest surprises in the history of American television.

When it was launched in 1969, *Sesame Street* was conceived as a tool for helping culturally deprived children between the ages of three and five. Its format featured animated film clips interspersed with live skits. The teachers included a motley crew of puppets called Muppets, among whom were Big Bird, a goggle-eyed creature known as Cookie Monster and a testy, woolly lump called Oscar the Grouch, who resided inside a garbage can. Viewers

were taught the basic skills of reciting the alphabet, counting to 10 and recognizing such simple forms as circles and triangles. Instruction in these skills plus practical lessons in everyday living were implemented by the use of eye-catching visual aids, displayed against an urban background.

The program succeeded far beyond expectations. Within a few years nine million children from all economic levels regularly watched it. It was soon being televised in 50 other countries, and original versions were shown in German, Spanish and Portuguese.

The purpose of helping disadvantaged children appears to have been handsomely fulfilled. One study showed the learning skills of such viewers had been sharpened by up to 62 per cent.

For the benefit of viewers who are learning to count, Big Bird points out an oversized number atop a street sign on a Sesame set.

In a lively session of alphabet instruction, four Sesame Streeters, singing and dancing, put together the letter "H."

"One of these things is not like the other," sings a cast member, pointing to four objects. A tot correctly fingers the egg.

Hamming it up, two Muppets try to pantomime the meaning of "love" and to add the word to the TV viewers' vocabulary.

In Luis' Fix-It Shop, Sam the Robot learns how to repair a juicer, then carefully repeats the steps for listening tykes.

The concepts of hot and cold are demonstrated by a pair of Sesame Street performers decked out in winter and summer costumes.

and metallurgy, among other fields. As an invention and economic product it has a history. As a sociological entity it has influenced American
life. "The youngster will learn more from the hot rod," Holt insists, "including how to make a living, than he would from the standard
compartmentalized courses in a traditional high school."

Schools that successfully apply such freewheeling methods are few—in
the United States, or elsewhere. Many observers fear they will always be
scarce, and are pessimistic about a reorganization of education in America and other countries on the scale attempted in Britain. James D.
Koerner, author and educator, believes that the United States simply does
not have an adequate supply of teachers good enough to run open classrooms successfully. "Ours is a mass system," Koerner says, "you can't
transplant the British methods unless you have sufficient teachers of comparable ability." Since U.S. teachers are often not as well trained as their
English counterparts, Koerner maintains, "carefully structured methods
in elementary schools will produce better results because the child's learning depends as much upon the material and drill as on the quality of the
person doing the teaching." Even so, Koerner favors imaginative teaching
and flexible curricula in the United States: "Let us by all means," he says,
"involve the student as actively as possible in the learning process."

The solution to many education problems, in Koerner's view, is better
education of teachers. In his book, *The Miseducation of American Teachers,* he puts the blame largely on the teachers' colleges. Among their worst
faults, he says, is too much emphasis on *how* to teach and too little on *what*
to teach—on the subjects that must be presented to students. The intel-

lectual quality of most American teachers' college courses in English or physics or other academic subjects he brands "inferior." As for the courses in teaching technique, they are "most often puerile, repetitious, dull and ambiguous." Many of these inadequacies he blames on the professionals who run the teachers' colleges. They are, Koerner says, "sincere, humanitarian, well-intentioned, hard-working," but too many of them are also "poorly informed, badly educated, and ineffectual."

The crucial role of teachers is suggested by the success of the French educational system in producing cultivated men and women. It indicates that a rigid, even grimly serious, program of studies can work when operated by well-trained teachers. And the good results of a quite different system, the British open schools, can also be attributed at least in part to the fact that England's teachers are by and large well schooled and dedicated to their jobs. Gifted teachers can apparently make almost any style of instruction work. In Germany, Ute Moeller-Andresen *(pages 160-169)* combines the open-school approach with more formal drill and memorization work. Her pupils learn perhaps because of the goals she sets for herself: to teach the children to be alive and curious, to demonstrate that it is one of life's great pleasures to satisfy that curiosity, and above all to free herself "from the ingrained rituals of teaching and put the children first, not the curriculum."

Neither Mrs. Andresen nor any other good teacher is under the illusion that school can be all play or that the children can, without guidance, educate themselves. Certain basic skills such as the multiplication tables must be learned through hard work and, yes, boring repetition. The teachers in the British open schools do not let their pupils play aimlessly but circulate ceaselessly in their classrooms, guiding and helping—and sometimes prodding—the children. But it does mean that the message that echoes through the centuries from Vittorino, Comenius, Pestalozzi, Froebel, Dewey and such contemporary critics as Holt and Silberman should be heeded—schools to be effective must be humane, must care for the individual pupil, should strive to make the school experience as pleasurable and purposeful as possible.

Given such conditions, even such a severe critic of today's schools as John Holt says that the miracle of learning can take place—if the teacher encourages thinking, gives confidence to the fearful, draws out the seemingly backward and demonstrates how the tasks that are assigned to the students are both connected and meaningful. "With luck," Holt says, "we can give some of them a feeling of what it is like to turn one's full intelligence on a problem, to think creatively, originally, and constructively instead of defensively and evasively." Psychological research into learning has helped educators come closer than ever before to an understanding of how the learning process operates. Now the schools and teachers must strive to apply this new-found knowledge to increase their effectiveness —and build a generation that can take better advantage of man's greatest inheritance, the ability to learn.

Strategies of a gifted teacher

In 1973 a book titled *The First School Year* was published in Stuttgart, Germany. The work of a young teacher named Ute Moeller-Andresen, it documented the technique she employs in teaching the first grade at a Munich public school. The book attracted wide attention and won glowing reviews, one of which suggested that it might be the basis "for a new and better school."

The teaching philosophy expounded by Mrs. Andresen combines contemporary and old-fashioned methods. She believes in discipline, and she teaches such standard subjects as arithmetic, writing and spelling. But she does not use textbooks; she instructs by practical, real-life examples instead. When she wants to explain fractions to the class, for example, she has them cut potatoes into quarters for vegetable soup.

Trained in psychology as well as pedagogy, Mrs. Andresen encourages each child to learn at his own pace. Throughout the year she tries to allay the anxieties that beset most six-year-olds: their fear on entering school that the other children are potential rivals, their ignorance of their bodies and the pains of growing up, their unfamiliarity with the busy city around them.

Above all, Mrs. Andresen wants her pupils to learn to enjoy being part of the group. No one is allowed to remain outside it; the faster learners are encouraged to help the slower ones, and everyone is exposed to the satisfactions of working as a team. Pupils and parents approve her approach. One mother commented: "The entire class loved going to school. She was teaching her pupils the kind of social integration that resulted in their becoming inspired, cooperative and positive."

While doing a spelling exercise, Mrs. Andresen's class sits in a horseshoe arrangement, enabling her to observe them unobtrusively.

A lesson meant to banish fears

In keeping with her philosophy that classroom instruction should relate as closely as possible to real-life problems, Mrs. Andresen gives her first-graders lessons in tooth care at just about the time they are starting to lose their baby teeth. Simultaneously, many of the children pay their first visits to the dentist, whose drills and lamps loom frighteningly above them. "These are major events for a six-year-old," she says, "and they want explanations. That makes teeth an ideal subject. By learning how the body works, a child loses his dread of physical injury or disintegration. His knowledge is a magic formula that is able to banish fears."

Aided by a diagram behind her showing a cavity in a tooth, Mrs. Andresen urges regular visits to a dentist to help spot holes while they are still small.

In a make-believe visit to the dentist, one little girl plays the patient while another, helped by an assistant holding a dental mirror, pretends to pull a tooth.

Asked to draw pictures of their own teeth for an art assignment, the children made this gallery of grinning portraits on wrapping paper with wax crayons.

Learning how to stop decay, a pupil brushes away during an exuberant class exercise that followed the showing of a film on the development and care of teeth.

The community as classroom

Mrs. Andresen often uses the Munich community to bring lessons home to the class. For example, she began a project on how food is made by growing wheat in a flowerpot and later grinding flour from the kernels. Then she took the children to a bakery *(right)* to see the wheat transformed into bread.

To learn how food can be preserved, her youngsters visited a local supermarket and noted ways in which vegetables are kept fresh *(below, right)*. And when some sessions on transportation led to consideration of the problems that arise when everyone drives his own car, the class acted out a solution on a city sidewalk *(below)*: they "took a bus."

Almost at the end of a course on how food is manufactured from raw material, the class watches a baker dust his rolls before putting them in the oven. In the last step, each pupil samples a fresh roll.

Encountering some cellophane-wrapped potatoes in a market, a pupil ponders whether their freshness has been preserved because they have been dried, frozen or sealed off from the air.

Chairs drawn together in orderly rows (left), the children tumble about in a pretense of riding on a bus. The lesson: though crowded, buses pollute the air less than the autos that jam Munich streets.

Becoming members of the team

The chief lesson Mrs. Andresen wants to impart is an appreciation of the value of working as a group. To do so, she uses the techniques shown here.

When a newcomer enters the class, she stages introductory sessions, like the one below. To acquaint everybody with the shared feeling that often springs up among members of a group—and, in the process, to educate the youngsters about the problems of mass-production labor—she organizes them into an assembly line and gives them a mutual task to perform *(right)*. And to help those who have an innate fear of physical contact, she teaches the class to play a hugging game *(bottom, right)*.

To arouse friendly interest in a new boy, Mrs. Andresen invited him to bring his cat to school. Below, master and pet enjoy the limelight as the children compare the cat's anatomy with a human's.

Learning about assembly-worker alienation, the class forms a line to produce paper ships. Each child was told to make only one fold or to insert one staple in a sheet, which was handed down the line. By the 20th ship, the children discovered that work gets sloppy when the people doing it are bored.

Embracing one another in a game called Goosethief, the class forms a circle around one child, who plays the thief. But even the thief is brought into the group, for after the circle goes round, everyone rushes to the center to hug him.

Confident and close-knit, Mrs. Andresen's class endures the annual ritual of having its picture taken as the end of their first year in school approaches. By now, she says, they are "real school children, speaking classroomese, with shared experiences, sure of their ability to learn. School is a valued part of their lives."

Bibliography

Auerbach, Erich, *Mimesis*. Princeton University Press, 1953.

Babkin, Boris P., *Pavlov: A Biography*. University of Chicago Press, 1949.

Bate, Walter J., *The Achievement of Samuel Johnson*. Oxford University Press, 1965.

Beals, Alan R., with George and Louise Spindler, *Culture in Process*. Holt, Rinehart & Winston, Inc., 1967.

Birmingham, Stephen, *The Right People*. Little, Brown & Co., 1968.

Blair, Clay, Jr., *Survive*. Medallion Books, 1973.

Boyd, William, *The History of Western Education*. Adam & Charles Black, 1952.

Brown, Roger, *Social Psychology*. The Free Press, 1965.

Bruner, Jerome S., *On Knowing*. Harvard University Press, 1962.

Cole, Michael, John Gay, Joseph A. Glick, and Donald W. Sharp, *The Cultural Context of Learning and Thinking*. Basic Books, Inc., 1971.

Cole, Michael, and Sylvia Scribner, *Culture & Thought*. John Wiley & Sons, Inc., 1974.

Dickens, Charles, *Hard Times*. The New American Library, Inc., 1961.

Dollard, John, and Neal E. Miller, *Personality and Psychotherapy*. McGraw-Hill Book Co., 1950.

Ellmann, Richard, *James Joyce*. Oxford University Press, 1959.

Forster, E. M., *Abinger Harvest*. Meridian Books, 1955.

Gay, John, and Michael Cole, *The New Mathematics and An Old Culture*. Holt, Rinehart & Winston, Inc., 1967.

Glasser, William, *Schools Without Failure*. Harper & Row Publishers, Inc., 1969.

Goulet, L. R., and Paul B. Baltes, eds., *Life-Span Developmental Psychology*. Academic Press, Inc., 1970.

Halacy, Daniel S., Jr., *Man and Memory*. Harper & Row Publishers, Inc., 1970.

Hilgard, Ernest, with Richard and Rita Atkinson, *Introduction to Psychology*, 5th ed. Harcourt Brace Jovanovich, Inc., 1971.

Holt, John, *How Children Fail*. Pitman Publishing Corporation, 1964.

Isaacs, Harold R., *India's Ex-Untouchables*. John Day Company, Inc., 1965.

Jonas, Gerald, *Visceral Learning*. Viking Press, Inc., 1973.

Kagan, Jerome, *Understanding Children*. Harcourt Brace Jovanovich, Inc., 1971.

Kagan, Jerome, and Ernest Havemann, *Psychology: An Introduction*. Harcourt Brace Jovanovich, Inc., 1972.

Kazin, Alfred, *A Walker in the City*. Harcourt, Brace & World, 1951.

King, Edmund J., *Other Schools and Ours*. Rinehart & Company, Inc., 1960.

Kinkade, Kathleen, *A Walden Two Experiment*. William Morrow & Company, Inc., 1973.

Kleemeier, Robert W., ed., *Aging and Leisure*. Oxford University Press, 1961.

Kleppner, Otto, *Advertising Procedure*, 5th ed. Prentice-Hall, Inc., 1966.

Koerner, James D., *The Miseducation of American Teachers*. Houghton Mifflin Co., 1963.

Koestler, Arthur, *Act of Creation*. Dell Publishing Co., Inc., 1966.

Kozol, Jonathan, *Death at an Early Age*. Houghton Mifflin Co., 1967.

Letter to a Teacher. The Schoolboys of Barbiana, Random House, Inc., 1970.

Lorayne, Harry, and Jerry Lucas, *The Memory Book*. Stein & Day, 1974.

Luria, Alexander R., *The Mind of a Mnemonist*. Basic Books, Inc., 1968.

Malson, Lucien, and Jean Itard, *Wolf Children*. Monthly Review Press, 1972.

Mead, Margaret, *New Lives for Old*. William Morrow & Company, Inc., 1956.

Meyer, Adolphe E., *An Educational History of the Western World*. McGraw-Hill Book Co., 1972.

Moeller-Andresen, Ute, *Das Erste Schuljahr*. Ernst Klett Verlag, 1973.

Norman, Donald A., *Memory and Attention*. John Wiley & Sons, Inc., 1968.

Orwell, George, *A Collection of Essays*. Harcourt Brace Jovanovich, Inc., 1953.

Piaget, Jean, *Psychology of Intelligence*. Littlefield, Adams & Co., 1960.

Proust, Marcel, *Remembrance of Things Past*. Random House, Inc., 1934.

Pulaski, Mary Ann Spencer, *Understanding Piaget: An Introduction to Children's Cognitive Development*. Harper & Row Publishers, Inc., 1971.

Russell, Bertrand, *The Autobiography of Bertrand Russell 1872-1914*. Little, Brown & Co., 1967.

Seligman, Martin E. P., and Joanne Hanger, *Biological Boundaries of Learning*. Meredith Corporation, 1972.

Silberman, Charles E., *Crisis in the Classroom*. Random House, Inc., 1970.

Skinner, B. F:
Beyond Freedom and Dignity. Alfred A. Knopf, Inc., 1971.
Walden Two. Macmillan, 1960.

Spicer, Dorothy, *Yearbook of English Festivals*. H. W. Wilson, 1954.

Talland, George A.:

Deranged Memory: A Psychonomic Study of the Amnesic Syndrome. Academic Press, Inc., 1965.
The Hampton Album. The Museum of Modern Art, 1966.

Turnbull, Colin M., *The Forest People.* Simon & Schuster, Inc., 1961.
Warner, W. Lloyd, *A Black Civilization.* Harper & Row Publishers, Inc., 1964.

Watson, John B.:
Behaviorism. University of Chicago Press, 1962.
Psychological Care of Infant and Child. Arno Press, 1972.

Picture Credits

Index

Numerals in italics indicate a photograph or drawing of the subject mentioned.

force, 115; of Manus of Admiralty Islands, 110; outside influences on, 110; of Palauans of Caroline Islands, 107-109, 117; and perspective, 103; of pre-Communist China, 107; primitive mind theory of, 104, 120, 121; of Pygmies of Africa, 103, 120; skills of, 104; space concepts in, 109-110; subcultures in, 110-117; of technological societies, 109; of Tikopia of Polynesia, 110; time concepts in, 109-110; traditions of, 104, 107, 110, *111-113*, 114; of Ulithians of Caroline Islands, 109, 117; values of, 104, 105-109, 110; and ways of thinking, 120-121
Culture and Thought, Cole and Scribner, 103
Culture in Process, Beals, 108

D

Darwin, Charles, 66; theory of evolution of, 66
Death at an Early Age, Kozol, 139
Deconditioning, 35, 37
Déjà vu, 85
Della Mirandola, Giovanni Pico, *18*; achievements of, 18
Demoiselles d'Avignon, Les (painting), Picasso, *67*
Dewey, John, 145-148
Dickens, Charles, 145
Diderot, Denis, *19*; achievements of, 19
Dimension(s), understanding of, 75
Disequilibrium, of mind, 80-81
Distortion, of memory, 98, 100-101
Dodson, John D., 46-47
Dog(s): conditioning of, 34; learning ability of, 8; Pavlov's experiments with, 34; training of, *38-39*
Dollard, John, 47, 49
Dolphin(s): language of, 11; learning ability of, 9-11
Douglas-Home, Sir Alec, *86*, 87
Dream(s), and memory, 89-90, 98
Drive, 34
Duke, Angier Biddle, *93*

E

Earthworm, learning ability of, 8
Edison, Thomas, 101
Edman, Irwin, 87, 101
Education, 135-159; for all children, 137, 141, 142, 144; in ancient Greece, *136*; approaches to, 136-137; authoritarian, 148-150; in boarding schools of England, 150; in Britain, 135, 136, 137, *138*, 139, *143, 146-147*, 150, 152-153, 159; Bruner's theories on, 153-155; Comenius' ideas on, 142, 144, 159; contact curriculum in, 155; controversies about, 135-137, 148; John Dewey's approach to, 145-148, 159; emphasis of, on grades, 140, 150; faults of, 97, 137-141, 148-152; fear of failure in, 137-

139; Vittorino da Feltre's philosophy of, 141, 159; in France, 137, 148-150, 159; free, 137; Froebel's theories on, 144, 159; in Germany, 135, 137, *160-169*; in Italy, 135, 137, 139-141; in Japan, 135; as living, organic process, 144; Horace Mann's philosophy of, 145; in Massachusetts, 145, 151-152; meaninglessness of, 139; methods of, 136-137; Montaigne's ideas on, 141-142; mutilation of spirit by, 139; in Niger, *154-155*; in open classrooms, *146-147*, 152-153, 155-158, 159; in Orient, 137; permissive, *143*; Pestalozzi's approach to, 142-144; Piaget's contribution to, 153; popular concern for, 135; in progressive schools, 148; in Prussia, 145; quality of, 135, 137; reading in, 158, 159; by *Sesame Street*, *156-157*; of slower students, 137, 139-141; in Soviet Russia, *134*, 135, 137; with teaching machines, *151*; with television, *154-155, 156-157*; three-level system of, 137; in United States, 135, 137-139, *140*, 141, 145, *149*, 150-152, 155-158; Wilderspin's approach to, 144-145
Eidetic imagery, 85
Einstein, Albert, 80
Elephant(s), learning ability of, 8
Enculturation, 104
Environment, 21, 34, 103, 104, 107
Equilibrium, of mind, 80-81
Erikson, Erik, 139
Eskimos, 109
Eton, 150
Exploration, 24

F

Fear, conditioned, *35*, 36
Feltre, Vittorino da, 141
First School Year, The, Moeller-Andresen, 160
Flemish, as subculture, 114
Flea(s), learning ability of, 8
Folk tales, 18
Forest People, The, Turnbull, 103
Forgetting, 84
Formal operational period, *76*, 77
Forster, E. M., 150
Fox, Logan J., 52
Free association, 98
Freud, Sigmund, 98
Froebel, Friedrich, 144

G

Gardner, Allen and Beatrice, 8
Gay, John, 103-104
Gieseking, Walter, 85-86
Glasser, William, 139
Glucksberg, Sam, 47
Goethe, Johann Wolfgang von, *19*; achievements of, 19
Greece, ancient: education in, *136*; memory

aids in, 92
Guadalcanal, in Solomon Islands, 105
Guilt, and memory, 98

H

Haber, Ralph, 85
Habit(s), harmful, 49
Hampton Institute, *118-119*
Harlem Prep, 155
Harrow, 150
Harvard Graduate School of Education, 151-152
Height, concept of, 71
Heredity, 34, 43-46
Hierarchies of memory, 101
High Society, 115
Hilgard, Ernest, 97
Hitler, Adolf, 44
Holmes, Oliver Wendell, 21
Holt, John, 137-139, 155-156, 159
Home learning, 20-21; importance of, 20-21; of spoken language, 20
Homer, 18
Honeybee, learning ability of, 8
How Children Fail, Holt, 137
Hunger, 34
Hypnosis, 94

I

Iliad, 18
Imitation, learning by, *14*, 15, 69
Impediment(s), to memory, 87-89, 97
Incentive, 21
India, subcultures of, 114
India's Ex-Untouchables, Isaacs, 114
Indoctrination, cultural, 104-105, *118-119*
Infancy, learning in, *22-23*; conditioning in, *35*, 36-37
Inhibition(s), to learning, 46-47
Innate ideas, theory of, 21
Instinct(s), natural, and conditioning, 46
Instruction, direct, *16*, 17
Intellectual development: abstract period of, 68, 74-75, 121; accommodation in, 74-75; assimilation in, 74-75; cause and effect in, 68; concrete operational period of, 68, 74, 75, 121; constancy of volume, 71; in different cultures, 120-121; and disequilibrium, 80-81; and drive to learn, 81; and equilibrium, 80-81; first stage of, *22-23*, 68-69, *70*, 71; formal operational period of, *76*, 77; fourth stage of, 23, *26-27*, 68, 74-75, *76*, 77; imitation in, 69, *73*; language learning period of, 68, 69-74; memory in, 71; object constancy in, 68; Piaget's stages of, *22-27*, 65, 68-75, *70*, *72*, *75, 76*, 77; preoperational period of, *72*, *73*; second stage of, 23, *24-25*, 68, 69-74; sensorimotor intelligence period of, 68-69, *70*, 71; stages of, *22-27*, 64, 65, 68-75, *70*, *72*,

Printed in U.S.A.